Sake is more than just a drink for sushi night—it's aromatic, food-friendly, and endlessly sippable. Whether you're pairing it with pizza, roast chicken, or pasta Bolognese, sake brings unexpected joy to any table.

Everyday Sake makes this iconic Japanese beverage simple, delicious, and fun. Yoko Kumano and Kayoko Akabori—founders of Umami Mart in Oakland, California—have spent more than a decade selling, sipping, and teaching all things sake. They've answered every real-life question—Can I serve sake in a wine glass? Is hot sake a crime? Does it go with cheese? How long does an open bottle last?—and now they've distilled their real-world expertise into this approachable, illustrated guide.

Inside, you'll find everything you need to drink and serve sake with confidence: how to taste and talk about sake, read bottle labels and navigate menus, and perfectly pair sake with your favorite meals. Packed with expert insights, practical tips, and helpful visuals, this book is your go-to companion for discovering the joys of sake—any day of the week!

"A must-have, whether you are a sake beginner or a person with more koji knowledge. Yoko Kumano and Kayoko Akabori cover everything you want to know about sake and break it down so that it is easy to digest and fun to read! I will return to *Everyday Sake* again and again."

—Kenta Goto, owner of Bar Goto and Bar Goto Niban

"*Everyday Sake* is the guide I wish everyone had when discovering sake for the first time—warm, clear, and refreshingly unpretentious. Yoko and Kayoko bring both expertise and genuine joy to every page, breaking down technique and tradition in a way that feels effortless. This book doesn't just teach; it welcomes you, invites you to linger, to pour, to taste, and to be grateful for the everyday moments that Japanese sake makes brighter."

—Julia Momosé, chef and creative director at Kumiko and author of *The Way of the Cocktail*

"Kayoko and Yoko have created the definitive road map for readers of all experience levels to learn about sake of all types for every conceivable venue in concise, accessible, easy-to-reference illustrated chapters that provide the technical vocabulary and critical framework to select the ideal sake for your next gathering."

—Jim Meehan, author of *Meehan's Bartender Manual*

"Yoko and Kayoko have distilled the complexity of sake into pure joy—*Everyday Sake* is as refreshing and illuminating as the drink itself. Their passion and clarity remind me that mastery begins with curiosity, shared over a well-chosen glass."

—Aldo Sohm, sommelier and author of *Wine Simple* and *Wine Simple: Perfect Pairings*

"Yoko and Kayoko have a remarkable talent for making sake approachable for everyone. To have access to their aesthetic and knowledge in print makes this colorful book such a fun teaching tool and reference book all in one."

—Tanya Holland, award-winning chef and author of *California Soul*

"This is an absolutely definitive guide to the wide and wonderful world of sake! Covering process and production, art and science, this book makes sake accessible and enjoyable with colorful imagery and new ways to pair and serve. As fun as it is informative, *Everyday Sake* demystifies one of the greatest and most misunderstood beverages."

—Kyle Connaughton, chef/owner of Michelin three-star restaurant SingleThread

EVERYDAY SAKE

EVERYDAY SAKE

THE GO-TO GUIDE TO CHOOSING, PAIRING + SERVING

Yoko Kumano and Kayoko Akabori

Illustrations by Anders Arhoj

CLARKSON POTTER/PUBLISHERS | NEW YORK

CONTENTS

1. Understand

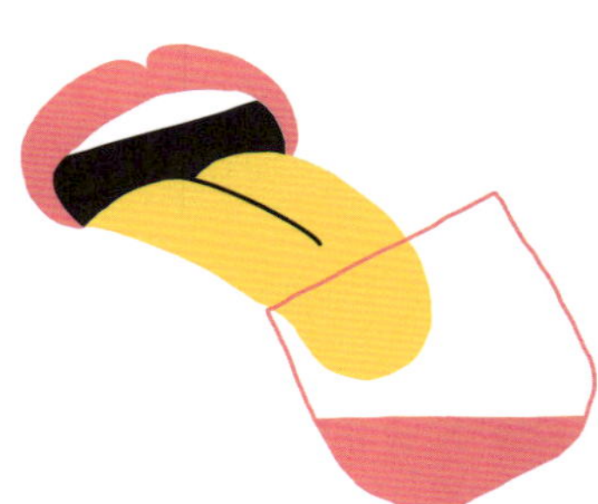

2. Taste

116

3. Choose

TO ALL
OF OUR
CUSTOMERS
PAST AND
PRESENT,
WHO KEEP
US GOING

ウマミ

INTRODUCTION

elcome to *Everyday Sake,* a handbook for answering all your burning questions about sake. Whether you are just embarking upon your sake journey or are already in it at full throttle, we hope this book will become your go-to guide on everything about this Japanese drink, from choosing and serving sake to enjoying, pairing, and storing it. Perhaps you are a wine lover or a gourmand looking to expand your palate and beverage horizons; maybe you are a beer brewer; or perhaps you have traveled to Japan and enjoyed sake there. No matter what your own experience has been, we wrote this book to meet you where you are, with real-life scenarios that we hear about every day in our sake shop in Oakland, California.

It is always our aim to get people to consider sake as an accompaniment for anything that they might be having for dinner, not just for sushi—from pasta and pizza to burgers and taco night. Thus spawned the idea for *Everyday Sake,* a book that invites sake into your life as an option alongside wine or beer. We consider sake to be an approachable, fuss-free drink that should not be reserved for special occasions or break the bank. As a bonus, premium sake is a nearly additive-free beverage—it is strictly regulated and can be made only with water, yeast, koji, and rice (read on, if you dare, for a possible fifth ingredient). Stabilizers or sulfites cannot be added for longer shelf life, like some wines, which makes sake an extremely transparent beverage. Although that may seem to mean sake is uncomplicated, the fact that you can extract such a wide range of flavors from so few ingredients is astonishing and thrilling.

We started selling sake in 2015, three years after opening our shop, Umami Mart, in downtown Oakland. At first, we specialized in Japanese barware, with the dream of eventually selling sake and other drinks from Japan. Once we obtained the necessary licenses for selling alcohol, we were off and running—and we have never looked back. We've become a sake destination for the Bay Area and beyond, and we have helped thousands of customers find bottles to enjoy at home or at a restaurant. Our sake club, Sake Gumi, has expanded our own knowledge of sake thanks to our monthly outreach and interviews with brewers and professionals in Japan. In 2019, we opened a bar inside the shop, where guests can unwind and learn more about sake. We take our role as stewards of sake culture seriously and are grateful for how much sake has enriched our own lives.

Just like wine and beer, sake is a fermented beverage meant to be paired with food or enjoyed on its own. It is highly aromatic, drinks wonderfully in a wine glass, and complements a variety of cuisines. It boasts a wide range of flavors and expressions: from extra dry to lusciously sweet, from crisp to as viscous as porridge, from transparent in hue to golden, which makes it pairable with all types of cuisines, from pizza and burgers to roasted chicken and pasta Bolognese.

So, think of *Everyday Sake* as a book that will act as a sake concierge for you: helping you choose the best sake for any dinner, gift, or special occasion, all while equipping you with some basic knowledge so you can confidently talk the sake talk.

HOW TO USE THIS BOOK

This book was created not as an intimidating tome, but as a way to help make serving and enjoying sake more practical in your daily life. With many years of selling sake under our belt, online and in real life, we are here to answer the questions you may have, like: Can I use a wine glass for sake? Is hot sake bad? Can I have cheese with sake? How long can I keep an opened bottle? You'll find the answers to all these questions and more here.

We reeled in our longtime friend and collaborator Anders Arhoj of Copenhagen to take you visually through the book in an imaginative yet relatable way. We hope that, as with any treasured cookbook or guidebook, you open this book often—go ahead and dog-ear it and make notes on its pages! Whether you are a novice or longtime sake lover, we want this book to be a trusty resource.

The book is organized into simple chapters that start with the fundamentals, then go on to practical tips and advice on how to taste, choose, pair, and serve sake. If you want to read the book from cover to cover, knock yourself out! We've peppered in some sidebars and other sections with extra information, tips, and how-tos. And charts! Boy, we've got charts. These are meant to make more complex information crystal clear and easy to digest. Let's do this!

ABOUT US

Hello! We're Yoko and Kayoko, founders of Umami Mart, a Japanese drinks store in Oakland, California. We were childhood friends growing up in Cupertino, and we reconnected through our love of food in our twenties when we were living on opposite sides of the globe (Yoko in Tokyo and Kayoko in Brooklyn). From our cramped cubicles, we started a food blog together (yup, called Umami Mart on Blogspot!), and from there, we both moved back to the Bay Area, where we dreamed of leaving our jobs and running Umami Mart full-time.

Kayoko

Through our visits to countless sake breweries all over Japan and the U.S., hundreds of tastings with importers and distributors, and daily conversations with our customers, we were able to collectively curate what is now one of the best sake selections in the country. More importantly, we are able to talk about every bottle on our shelves, and to make pairing and temperature suggestions according to our customers' own preferences. Umami Mart has become a destination for sake and tastings, where customers visit from far and wide to discover their next

Yoko

favorite bottle while chatting about their favorite places for ramen. (We have opinions: Perhaps try soba or udon instead!)

As a certified kikizakeshi (sake sommelier), Yoko has been the director of Umami Mart's sake program since 2015, meticulously stocking the shelves and leading our monthly Sake Gumi club with creative tasting notes, videos, and interviews with brewers. Yoko's sake journey began in Tokyo in 2006, when she had her first sip of Shinkame junmai. But it wasn't until 2010, when she took a job behind the sake-tasting counter at Takara Sake in Berkeley, that her love of sake blossomed. There she worked with Izumi Motai, whose infectious passion for everything sake, from izakaya history to koji, showed her that there was a whole wide world of sake out there for her to learn about. Her journey as a sake student continues as she follows the makers who inspire her, including Miho Imada of Imada Shuzo and Keizo Ishida of Matsuse Shuzo.

Kayoko's deep appreciation of sake is thanks to her dad, who is a self-proclaimed "Junmai Guy" and arbiter of all things sake. After spending the 2000s in New York, eating and drinking her way through the city and blogging about it, she returned to the Bay Area to bartend at Camino, a restaurant in Oakland. While Kayoko is Umami Mart's shochu director, she regularly tags along with Yoko to visit sake breweries in Japan, edits all the club tasting notes, and writes about aruten sake and aged sakes for the club. Honjozos are her jam.

酒

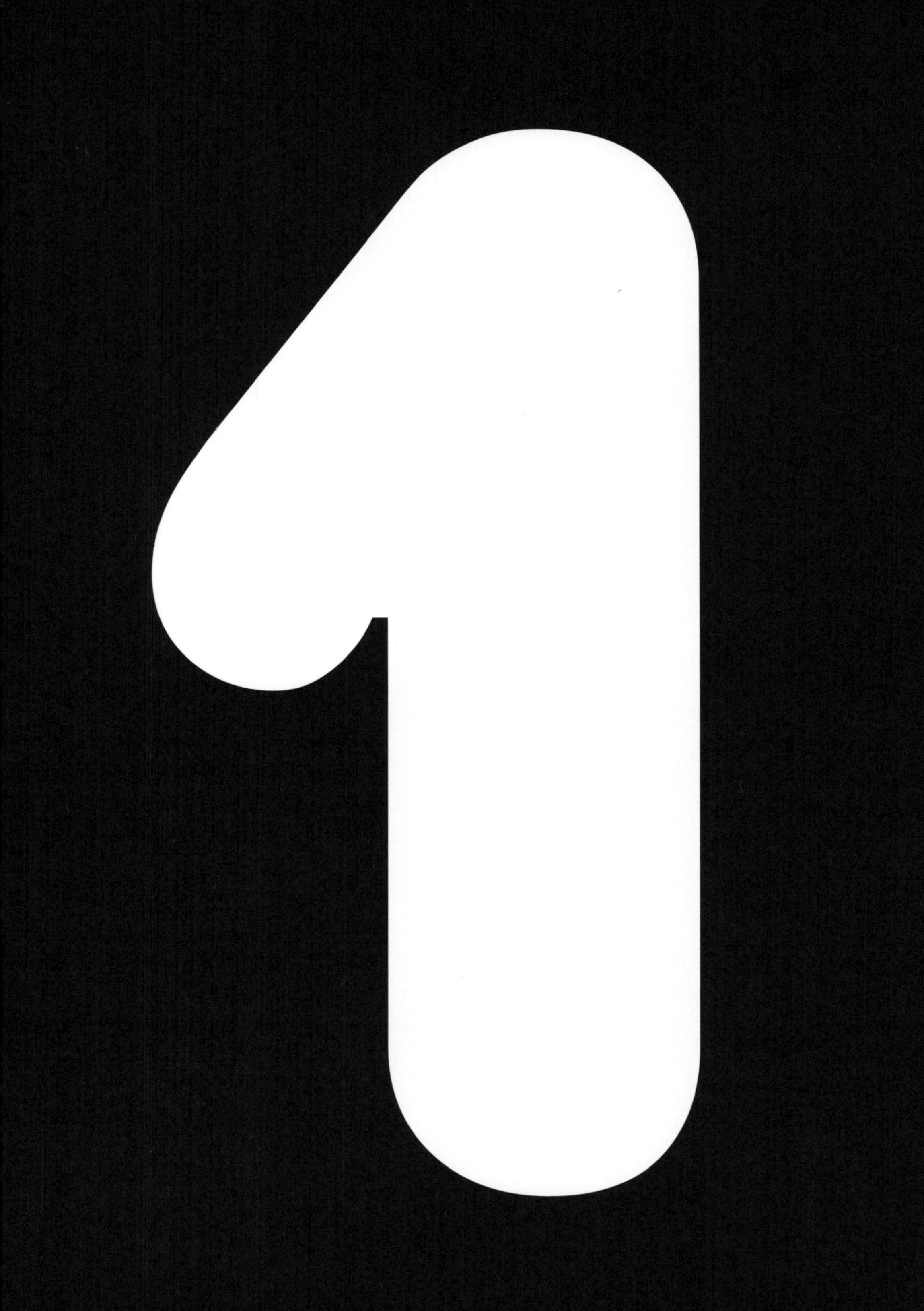

UNDERSTAND

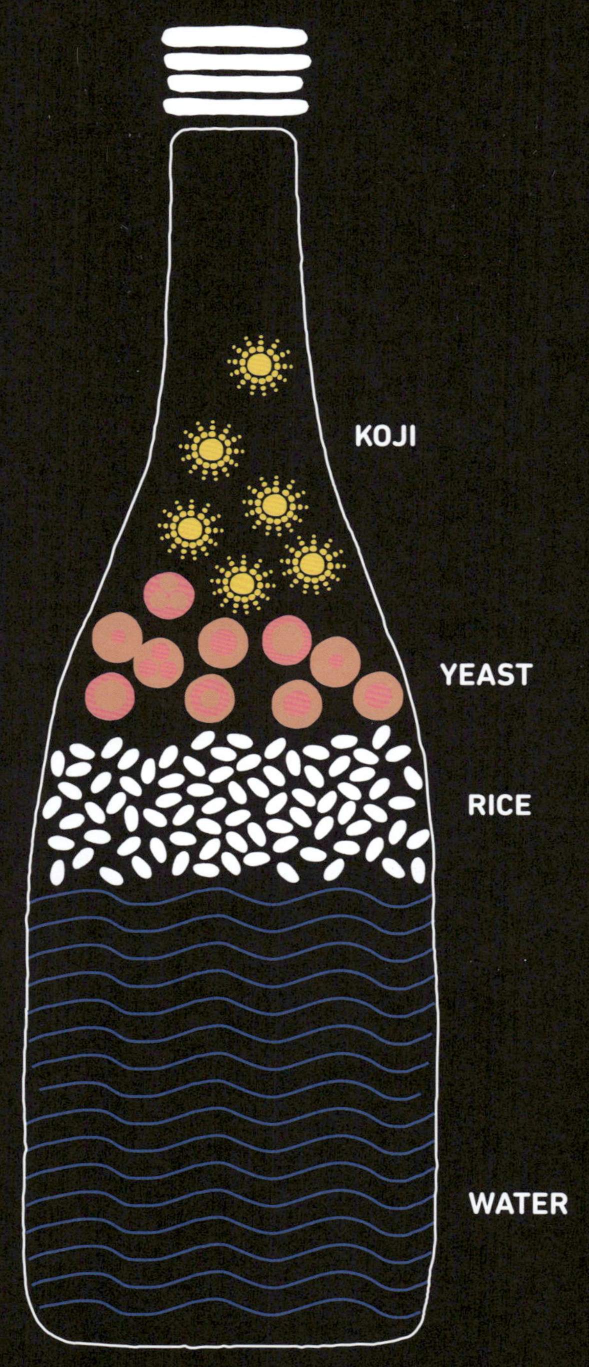
KOJI
YEAST
RICE
WATER

WHAT IS SAKE?

Sake is a fermented alcoholic beverage made from rice. Native to Japan, it was first made roughly 1,700 years ago in the fourth century, when rice cultivation (introduced to Japan from China) was in full swing.

Sake is made with rice, water, yeast, and koji (a type of mold), but it may also have distilled alcohol added to it. It has a slightly higher alcohol level than wine, at about 15%. Like wine, it's best sipped or paired with food. However, since sake is made from a grain, it also shares some characteristics with beer.

Yet, although it shares some characteristics with other beverages, sake is sake. It is unique and in its own category.

Sake is not wine.

Wine is an alcoholic beverage fermented from fruit. Because sake is fermented from a grain (rice), it is not wine. You may see it mislabeled as "rice wine." But wine can technically be made only from fruit, and therefore, the name "rice wine" is misleading.

Sake is not a spirit. Spirits are made by distilling fermented beverages. As sake is not distilled, it is not a spirit.

Sake is not beer. Beer is a fermented beverage that can be made from different types of grain. It typically uses the malting process for germination and subsequent saccharification (turning grain starch into usable sugars for the yeast's consumption). Although you can make a beer with rice, you cannot make sake with any grain other than rice. Additionally, you must use koji when making sake.

If you ever have trouble remembering how to pronounce *sake*, just think of *Everyday Sake*! *Sake* is pronounced "sa-kay," not "sa-kee."

HOW SAKE IS MADE

Since sake is made with only up to five ingredients, great care goes into preparing each one.

Before we go deep into exploring those five ingredients, let's talk about alcohol fermentation. For wine, beer, and sake, fermentation is the process of turning an organic grain or fruit into alcohol by using the power of microorganisms. All three require yeast, a microorganism to convert the sugars from the grain or fruit into alcohol. The grain used for beer (most commonly barley) and sake (rice) must undergo a process called saccharification. This is the conversion of grain starches into usuable sugars, which the yeast can then use as food to create alcohol. To saccharify grains for beer, brewers must malt (germinate) the grains and then mash them in hot water to make wort. To saccharify rice for sake, brewers use another microorganism called koji to convert rice starch into usable sugars for the yeast (please refer to page 24 for more on koji).

Alcohol fermentation for sake is especially unique because koji can saccharify rice at the same time as the yeast is converting sugars into alcohol. The chart opposite shows the three distinct fermentation processes for each beverage.

FERMENTATION METHOD COMPARISON

SIMPLE FERMENTATION (WINE)

MULTIPLE SEQUENTIAL FERMENTATION (BEER)

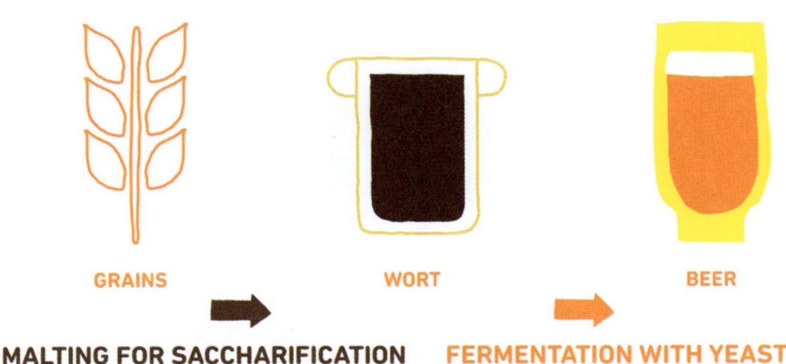

MULTIPLE PARALLEL FERMENTATION (SAKE)

Rice Type

Rice varieties for sake are considered in a different way from grape varieties for wine. While the variety of rice is important, the rice-polishing ratio is often more important, because that is what determines the type of sake. That said, one should not dismiss the rice varietal completely, as it can offer hints about the sake's characteristics and flavor profile. Although it's not a requirement, most breweries state the type of rice used on the label. Here are the top five sake rice varieties used today.

Rice variety	Prefecture where it is commonly grown	Sake types	Sake tasting notes	Other characteristics
Yamada Nishiki	Hyogo	Junmai daiginjo, daiginjo	Soft, round, floral, light fruit	Compact *shinpaku* (the concentrated starch in the center of the rice grain); ideal for polishing
Gohyakumangoku	Niigata	All premium grades, futsushu	Dry, refreshing, crisp	Larger shinpaku; harder to polish
Miyama Nishiki	Nagano	All premium grades, futsushu	Clean, light, sharp	Thrives in cold temperatures and high altitude
Omachi	Okayama	All premium grades	Herbal, earthy, layered	Oldest known sake rice variety; not crossbred
Akita Sake Komachi	Akita	All premium grades, futsushu	Elegant, soft, slight sweetness	Akita Prefecture's alternative to Yamada Nishiki

Ingredients

Water

A sake brewer must first choose a site for their brewery that has access to water suitable for the type of sake they wish to make. Water with a high mineral content of magnesium, potassium, and phosphorus will provide more nutrients for the yeast, which can result in a livelier fermentation for strong, bold styles of sake. However, some brewers prefer low levels of these minerals for a slow and low temperature fermentation, resulting in a more delicate sake. Iron is undesirable in water used for making sake—it can result in colors and aromas that are off.

Rice

Then the brewer must choose the best variety of rice and the optimal polish for the type of sake they want to produce. The type of sake they are making may determine the variety they use. For example, many daiginjos are made with Yamada Nishiki because the rice is suited for polishing. The region where the sake is made can also influence the sake rice chosen. Brewers in Nagano are known to use Miyama Nishiki because it grows well in its cold climate. The rice variety can also affect the flavor of the sake. This is often demonstrated in sakes made with Omachi, which express herbal characteristics.

Yeast

Yeast selection is important in sake-making because when the koji converts rice starches into sugars, the yeast converts those sugars into alcohol. In the process, the yeast produces carbon dioxide, amino acids, and esters. Brewers choose different types of yeasts for their stamina, behaviors at different temperatures, aroma, and types of acids they produce.

Most sakes are made using yeast purchased from the Nihon Jozo Kyoukai (Brewing Society of Japan). The Brewing Society of Japan produces and sells yeast to sake-makers in Japan and around the world. The yeasts that have been isolated and cultivated by this society are numbered.

But some brewers use yeasts that are proprietary, prefectural, ambient (yeasts living in the brewery), associated with a particular region, or uniquely their own. For example, some breweries isolate yeasts from flowers or fruit. Using proprietary yeasts can set a sake apart from any other sakes on the market. These sakes may also express flavors and aromas most people have never experienced before. We are seeing more breweries using unique yeasts, including yeasts from olives, honey, and wine, to stand out from the rest.

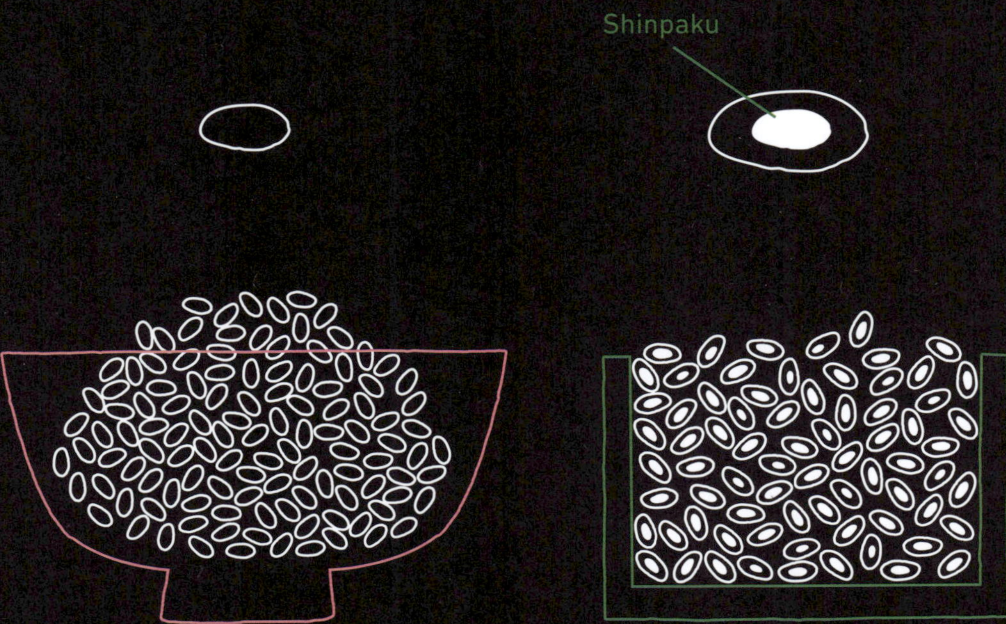

Rice You Eat Versus Sake Rice

The rice we eat at the dinner table differs from the rice used for sake-making. The grains of sake rice are about 30% bigger than the rice we buy in the store. Sake rice is also softer than table rice so that it can absorb more water during soaking and steaming. And while the rice we eat has a mix of proteins, lipids, minerals, and starch distributed throughout the grain, the makeup of a grain of sake rice is unique. Ideally, the grain has a well-defined starch center (*shinpaku*), with the proteins, lipids, and minerals surrounding it. That allows you to control the amount of proteins, lipids, and minerals that are polished off, which will affect the flavor of the sake. Generally speaking, the more of the outer layers you retain, the bolder or richer the sake will taste. During the fermentation process, the starchy center is broken down into usable sugars for the yeast to convert into alcohol.

While people have been making sake since the fourth century, cultivating sake rice didn't come onto the scene until the early 1900s. The most popular sake rice used today, Yamada Nishiki, was produced in 1936 at the Hyogo Prefectural Agricultural Research Center, where they crossbred Yamadaho and Tankan Wataribune, two heirloom sake rice types. Yamada Nishiki is prized for having a well-defined starch ball and low protein content.

Koji Chronicles

Koji rice is rice inoculated with koji spores, which are used to make sake, shochu, soy sauce, mirin, and miso. There are three main types of koji spores used in Japan—yellow, white, and black. For sake-making, the most common spores used are yellow koji (*Aspergillus oryzae*). The two other types are white (*Aspergillus Kawachii*) and black (*Aspergillus awamori*), which are used for *shochu* and *awamori* (distilled spirits from mainlaind Japan and Okinawa, respectively). However, in recent years, more sake brewers have been brewing with white and black koji, which express different acidity profiles in sake.

During the *moto* (fermentation starter) process, the koji develops enzymes that break starches into sugars. Then yeast is added to the moto to ferment the sugars into alcohol. The use of koji is what sets sake apart from other fermented beverages. When we ask various brewers about koji, their demeanor always softens, as though they are talking about their children. To brewers, koji is a living, breathing organism with unique characteristics that define the essence of their sake. While the yeast has an influence on the aroma of the sake, koji affects the core flavor of the sake—so much so that many brewers consider koji-making the most important part of sake-making, because it affects how umami is perceived in the final product.

Umami is a prized type of taste in sake, setting it apart from other alcoholic beverages that may exhibit more sweetness or acidity. And while beverages higher in acidity, like wine, can help "reset" your palate, umami is said to enhance the flavors of different ingredients. One of our greatest memories is visiting Kita Shuzo in Shiga to help make the koji used for our Umami Mart junmai. This koji is cultivated for fifty hours instead of the usual forty-eight, which contributes more depth of flavor—yes, more umami!

Koji

Finally, the brewer must select the kind of koji they will use. Yellow koji is the most common type used for sake-brewing. More rarely, some sake brewers may use white or black koji, which result in higher levels of citric acid. Because most brewers use yellow koji, it is the way they grow the koji spores on the rice grains that is the most significant factor here. This process involves sprinkling koji spores over steamed rice and then precisely controlling the temperature about forty-eight hours to minimize or maximize amino acid conversion. The careful adjustments the brewer makes to this process are how they dial in the final product.

Distilled Alcohol

An optional fifth ingredient in sake-making is a neutral spirit. For *futsushu* (ordinary) sakes, alcohol is added to increase yield. For premium sakes, it is added to enhance aroma or texture. In the latter case, brewers are limited to using a maximum of 10% of the weight of the rice used. It is speculated that shochu was traditionally used for this practice in the old days, but there is no restriction on what the alcohol is or where it comes from. Today most brewers use neutral spirits imported from South America.

Production

Now that we've reviewed the main ingredients for sake, let's discuss how sake is made.

Rice Preparation

Sake-making starts with the rice. First, it must be polished, washed, soaked, and steamed. Painstaking care goes into each step, especially if the brewer is making an ultrarefined sake such as a daiginjo. While many of the steps are mechanized today, some smaller-batch brewers opt to do everything by hand for more control.

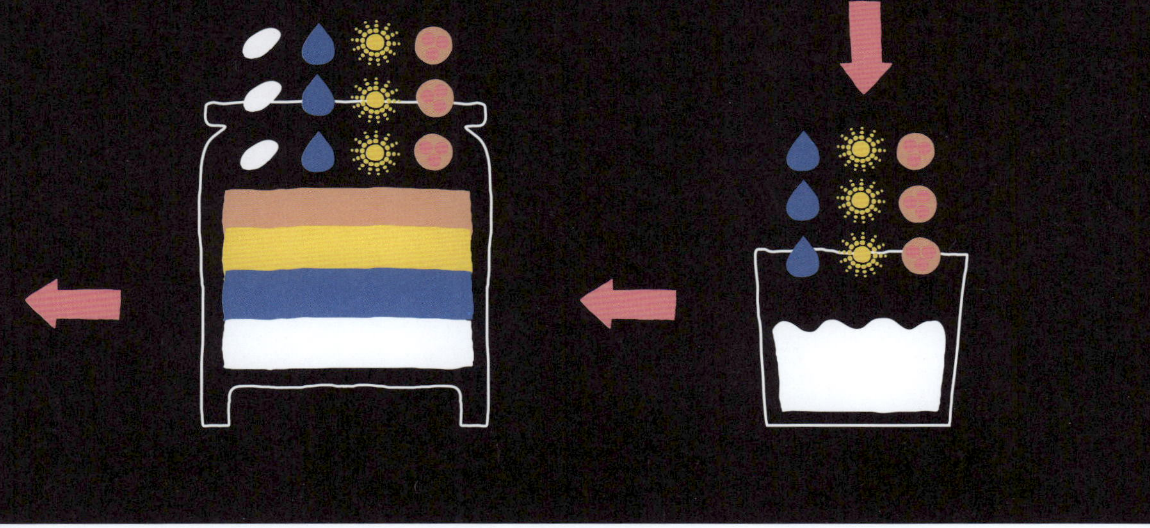

Koji Preparation

Every brewer has their own way of making koji—the main difference is whether they choose to make it by hand or with a machine. While most of the breweries we visit make their koji by hand, larger brewers use automated processes: Pipes and conveyer belts transfer the koji from one step to the next, and temperature control is regulated. Because we've more often seen koji made by hand, we describe the handmade process in this section. But the following steps must occur whether by hand or automated.

Koji-making starts after the rice has been freshly steamed in the morning. The steamed rice is first cooled and then taken into a humid enclosed space called a *koji muro* (koji room). The rice is spread out on a platform (a low wooden or steel "bed" with a large surface area) and koji mold spores are shaken onto the rice. It then takes about ten hours for the spores to inoculate the rice. Over these ten or so hours, brewers coddle the rice by wrapping it up in blankets to keep it warm and then breaking it apart for even growth. After this, the focus shifts from establishing mold growth to controlling how the mold grows onto each grain. Will the sake-maker opt for a *souhaze*-style koji growth pattern, which thoroughly covers the outer surface of the rice grain in addition to going deep into the grain with koji filaments for a richer, thicker style of sake? Or will they choose a *tsukihaze*-style koji growth, which results in sparse coverage on the surface and some filament growth inside the grains for a lighter, elegant style of sake?

The sake-maker will choose to spread the koji onto one large bed or onto medium-size boxes or small trays, depending on the growth pattern they wish to achieve. While large beds can yield more koji and are ideal for souhaze koji, small trays allow the sake-maker to control the temperature and humidity of the koji with more precision by shifting and moving the trays throughout the following seven to ten hours, which make the grains ideal for tsukihaze koji. The medium boxes can provide the brewer with an option in between, allowing them to control the process but without the constant monitoring that the small trays require. This option can produce a wide range of sake styles.

After this stage, the koji is removed from the koji room for drying. The koji is left in the drying room for about half a day and then transferred to the fermentation starter (*moto*) tank, where it is combined with rice and water. The entire process, from sprinkling the spores onto the rice to transferring it to the tank, takes about forty-eight hours.

Note: When we refer to koji in sake-making, we are talking about rice that has been inoculated with koji mold spores. The spores look like a fine greenish powder, and koji-inoculated rice looks like crumbly dried rice. A whole book could be written just about making koji!

Moto (Fermentation Starter)

After the rice and koji preparation, it's time to make the *moto,* or fermentation starter. The goal here is to create a safe environment for yeast to grow in the starter tank. The starter tank is about 10% of the size of the main fermentation tank. Typically rice, water, yeast, koji, and lactic acid are combined to create the starter. The lactic acid helps keep the starter acidic enough to kill any unwanted bacteria. It takes fourteen days to establish the starter using the common *sokujo* method (see chart).

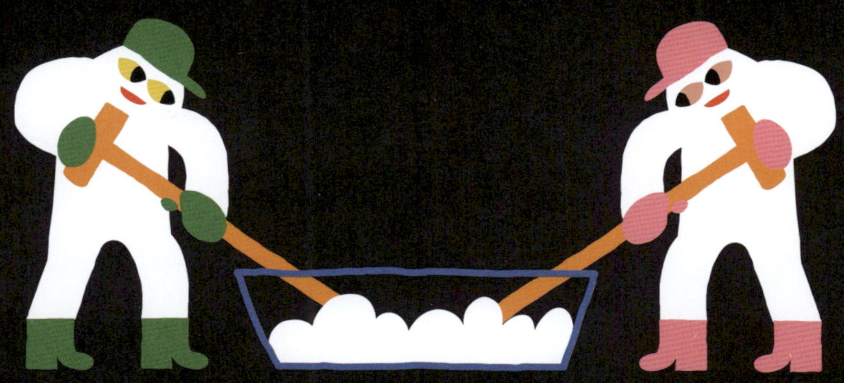

DIFFERENT MOTO (STARTER) METHODS

While 90% of sakes are made using the sokujo method, we are seeing more breweries releasing sakes made with traditional starter methods like kimoto, yamahai, and bodaimoto. The sokujo method is made with pure lactic acid and cuts the time for making a starter by half. The other, older methods create lactic acid naturally. While these methods take more time, brewers may use them to enhance acidity or bring out more rustic flavors in the sake. Here are some different starter methods at a glance.

Moto (starter)	Period	Total days for completion	Production characteristics	Common characteristics and flavors
Bodaimoto + mizumoto	Nara period (710–784)	10–13	Before working on the starter, brewers soak uncooked rice (and a little bit of steamed rice) in room-temperature water. The water harbors lactic acid. The raw rice is strained out from the acidic water, which is reserved, and cooked. The cooked rice and acidic water are then used in the starter, along with koji and yeast.	Acidic, yogurt, grapes, tart, earthy, aged cheese
Kimoto	1600s	28	Steamed rice, water, and koji are combined and pounded with a paddle into a mash. Lactic acid develops naturally, then yeast is added.	Acidic, nutty, bold, earthy
Yamahai	1909	28	Steamed rice, water, and koji are combined. Lactic acid develops naturally, then yeast is added.	Acidic, yogurt, umami, earthy
Sokujo-moto	Early 1900s	14	Steamed rice, water, and koji are combined. Once the koji has broken down the starches of the rice into sugars, lactic acid is added, followed by yeast.	Low acidity, light, refined

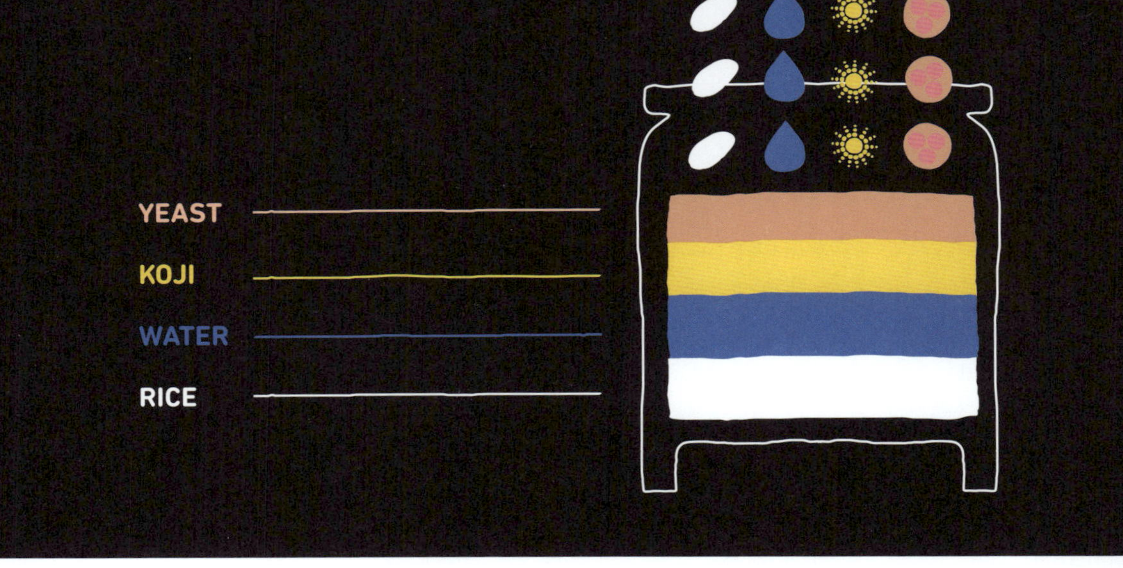

Moromi (Main Fermentation)

After the moto (starter) is complete, it is transferred to a tank that is about ten times the size of the starter tank and the main fermentation begins. The main mash (*moromi*) is created by adding rice, water, and koji three times over four days (this process, referred to as *sandan-jikomi,* is unique to sake-making). On day one, one-sixth of the total used rice (including the rice in the moto), water, and koji are added. On day two, the mixture is left alone for the yeast to build up. On the third day, one-third of the total used rice, water, and koji are added. On the fourth and final day, half of the total used rice, water, and koji are added.

The reason these ingredients are added at three different times throughout this period is to control the amount of food available to the yeast and to avoid smothering it. If everything was added all at once, the starch-to-sugar conversion and sugar-to-alcohol conversion would be thrown off-balance. Then, after the fourth day, the sake is left to ferment for another twenty to thirty days. The sake-making process up to this point usually takes forty-five to sixty days, depending on which starter method the brewer uses.

Post Fermentation

If the brewer wants to add distilled alcohol to the sake, they do it after fermentation. Otherwise, the sake is pressed immediately after fermentation. This separates the *sake kasu* (rice solids, or lees) from the clear liquid. The brewer may then choose to charcoal-filter the sake to remove unwanted yellowish tints or any odors that may be present (similar to passing water through a Brita filter).

Then the sake undergoes its first pasteurization. Sake typically goes through two heat pasteurizations: one after pressing and one right before shipping, both at a temperature between 60° and 65°C (140° and 149°F) for 10 to 30 minutes. There are two main reasons for pasteurizing sake. First, it stops active koji from creating enzymes that break down starches into sugars and the yeast from feeding on those sugars. This ensures that the sake remains stable and will have a longer shelf life. The second reason is for taste. While *namazakes* (unpasteurized sakes) can be vibrant and exciting, pasteurization can smooth out any rough edges.

After the first pasteurization, the sake is stored in tanks (storage time can vary, but it's typically three to six months) so the flavors mellow further. The sake is usually pasteurized again after storing. At this stage, the sake is still *genshu* or tank strength, and most brewers add water to bring the alcohol by volume (ABV) down to 15%. The very last step is bottling—and getting the sake into your hands!

DETERMINING SAKE TYPES

You can crack the code of sake types by understanding that it's all based on whether or not alcohol is added and how much the rice has been polished.

Ingredients

All sakes fall into one of two camps when considering the ingredients: junmai or aruten. Junmai sakes must be made with only rice, water, yeast, and koji, while aruten sakes have alcohol added to them before pressing. There is a wide range of flavors and characteristics within each camp—the chart below lists some of their key charateristics.

If a sake was made with only rice, water, koji, and yeast, you will see the word *junmai* (meaning "pure rice") on the bottle. If the label doesn't include the word, it means the brewer added distilled alcohol to the sake. In most cases, the alcohol is added to enhance the aromatics or give the sake a silkier texture. Sakes with added alcohol are referred to as *aruten*, but that term will not appear on the bottle.

	Junmai	**Aruten**
Ingredients	Rice, water, yeast, koji	Rice, water, yeast, koji, distilled alcohol
Aroma	Rustic, bold	Fragrant, alcohol
Taste	Rich, umami, acidic	Sweet, clean, bitter
Texture	Viscous, weighty	Light, silky
Indication on label	Junmai	None
Types included	Junmai, junmai ginjo, tokubetsu junmai, junmai daiginjo	Futsushu, honjozo, ginjo, daiginjo
Notes	Made with only four ingredients and considered *tokuteimeishoshu* (premium sake)	Futsushu sake can have additives like sugar, flavor enhancers, and acids and is not considered *tokuteimeishoshu* (premium sake); honjozo, ginjo, and daiginjo cannot have additives and are considered tokuteimeishoshu

Rice Polishing

The rice-polishing ratio refers to the amount of rice *remaining* in the sake. For example, a 70% rice-polishing ratio means that 30% of the outer portion of the rice has been removed and 70% remains.

Highly polished sakes are labeled *ginjo* or *daiginjo*. Ginjo sakes must be made with rice that has a polishing ratio of 60% or less; daiginjo sakes must use rice that has a polishing ratio of 50% or less. There is no rule about how low you can go. How much the rice is polished affects how refined or bold a sake tastes. The less that is removed from the outer portion of the rice grain, the bolder and earthier the sake. The more that is removed, the more subtle and delicate the sake.

To generalize, the higher the rice-polishing ratio, the bolder and richer the sake. The lower the rice-polishing ratio, the more delicate and softer the texture. With just this information, the world of sake will open up to you.

We've tried sake made from rice with a 100% rice-polishing ratio (i.e., unprocessed brown rice)—it was chewy, sour, and, frankly, a bit rough. On the other hand, we've tried sake made with a rice-polishing ratio of 1% (yes, they removed 99% of the outer portion of the rice)! This sake was so subtle, with faint hints of floral notes, that we felt as if we were sipping on the world's most expensive water. There is a reason why sake-makers often hover between the 60% and 70% rice-polishing ratio to brew a sake (these are usually identified as honjozo or junmai), as it balances out any extremes.

TRY IT! Try a bowl of brown rice, which has a rice-polishing ratio of 100% (i.e., totally unpolished), next to a bowl of white jasmine rice, which has a polishing ratio of 90%. How do they taste side by side? Now try a junmai sake with a rice-polishing ratio of 70% or higher next to a junmai daiginjo or daiginjo that has a rice-polishing ratio of 50% or lower. The comparisons are the same. The less polish, the more earthy, chewy, and nutty the sake can taste.

Typicity of Sake: An Evolving History

Typicity in wine is defined by how well a wine reflects the region it represents or the grape varietals it's made from. We like to refer to typicity of sake as how well the sake represents its type, which is determined by its ingredients or to what degree the rice being used is polished. Of the seven classic types we discuss here, futsushu is considered ordinary sake and all of the others are considered tokuteimeishoshu, or premium sake. We spoke with many sake-makers and winemakers about this topic.

Keizo Ishida, the head brewer of Matsuse Shuzo in Shiga, brought up the comparison of sake and wine. While it's not an apples-to-apples comparison, "You can use the Appellation d'Origine Contrôlée (AOC) of French wine as an example," he told us. "If futsushu is considered a vin de table, it would be realistic to compare tokuteimeishoshu to AOC-certified wine."

One difference to note between the Japanese classification of sake and wine is that "to get classified in the AOC, there is an actual taster who judges the typicity of the wine," said Chris Brockway of Broc Cellars in California.

While brewers can add large amounts of distilled alcohol and stabilizers to futsushu, ingredients for tokuteimeishoshu sake are restricted. These can have only a minimal amount of distilled alcohol added to them, must use a minimum of 15% koji, and are named according to the sake's rice-polishing ratio. A long history of grading and classifying sake predates this current system.

The previous grading system, called *kyubetsuseido*, did, in fact, require judges to determine the rice type. However, because under this system sake types were taxed differently, some makers deliberately didn't submit their sakes for classification. The tokuteimeishoshu system replaced kyubetsuseido in 1990. It is based on ingredients and rice-polishing ratios and was intended to be an objective system that did not rely on tasting or judging. But rice-polishing techniques have evolved since the 1990s and many brewers consider tokuteimeishoshu an outdated system.

Shuso Imada of the Japan Sake and Shochu Makers Association mentioned that discussions about a new system may be on the horizon, since some brewers don't list sake types on their labels and don't find the categorizations helpful. The answer is ultimately in the palate of the beholder, as we have found junmais that taste like daiginjos, and ginjos that taste like honjozos.

"It's good timing for a new system, and that discussion should be done," Imada said. Kazuki Odaira of the Midorikawa Sake Company in Niigata agreed, saying that while "the ingredient requirements still make sense, the rice-polishing ones do not and are a bit outdated." This has led some brewers to refuse to label their sakes for fear that their sakes will be typecast by their labels. This signals a growing protest against the current system.

In the meantime, while the tokuteimeishoshu grading system still reigns, its types stay relevant as they establish a standard for consumers in Japan and all over the world.

Era	System	Characteristics	Issues
Before 1990	Kyubetsuseido	A government entity judged sakes for quality and determined type.	Types were taxed differently, which resulted in sake-makers opting out of classification.
1990–present	Tokuteimeishoshu	Ingredients and rice-polishing ratio determine type.	Rice-polishing technology advancement has resulted in types that do not taste the same as they did when the system was established. Some sake-makers opt out of labeling their sakes as a type.
Future	Not yet determined	With outdated guidelines set by tokuteimeishoshu, breweries will tackle the issue of types with the changing times.	Potential confusion for the consumer as new guidelines will need to be defined.

The History of Aruten (Alcohol-Added) Sakes

Adding distilled alcohol to sake is a technique created during the Edo period (1603–1868) to fortify sakes and better preserve them for transport; the resulting sakes are called *aruten* sakes. Then, during World War II, it became law that all sake-makers must add distilled alcohol for bigger yields—because of the wartime rice shortage, it was forbidden to make junmai sakes (which require a lot of rice). But fortification got out of hand during the war. Sakes were being made with toxic substances like methanol, and people got sick. During wartime, depression and alcoholism were rampant, which also made these unregulated sakes especially dangerous.

In 1944, the government stepped in with new regulations. Sake-makers could now only fortify the yield of their sake with added distilled alcohol, sugars, stabilizers, and acids that totaled 100% of the weight of the rice used for making the sake. So if a brewer used 100 kg of rice to make their sake, the maximum combined weight of all the additives allowed would be 100 kg.

This type of sake, referred to as *sanzoshu* (which translates to "tripled sake" because combining additives usually resulted in three times the volume of the original), was popular well into the '60s, until both sake-makers and consumers started to demand better quality.

added to sake.

The 1970s saw further developments in alcohol-added sakes. Sanzoshus fell out of favor and futsushu sakes began to take their place. Futsushus are sakes that can have added distilled alcohol, sugars, stabilizers, and acids at up to 50% of the weight of the rice used for making the sake.

In 1990, *tokuteimeishoshus* (premium sakes) were officially recognized. These include honjozos, ginjos, and daiginjos, and these three types take the restrictions of aruten (added-alcohol) sakes more than a step forward by limiting the addition of distilled alcohol to no more than 10% of the weight of the rice used for making the sake. Additionally, sugars, stabilizers, and acids cannot be used for these premium sakes. So, why not get rid of added alcohol altogether? Brewers had found that adding alcohol was another tool for enhancing aroma, as certain aromas are soluble in alcohol.

In the 1980s, daiginjos and ginjos, which use highly polished rice, became showstoppers. The addition of alcohol came to be thought of as an "aroma booster." To this day, most of the sakes that are entered into competitions are daiginjos, thanks to their trademark silky mouthfeel and opulent aromas.

Why Is There No Minimum Rice-Polishing Ratio Set for Each Type?

There are many sake-makers who brew a junmai ginjo with rice polished to 50%—so why don't they call it a junmai daiginjo? It could be that the brewer has several sakes in the 50% rice-polishing range and wants to differentiate between them. For example, one sake may exhibit more floral characteristics and be called a junmai daiginjo, while another one that has more body and bright fruit notes will be called a junmai ginjo. Or it may be that the brewer calls their sake using 60% polished rice a junmai, their sake using 50% polished rice a junmai ginjo, and their sake using 40% polished rice a junmai daiginjo.

To understand the nuts and bolts behind the lack of minimum percentages, we consulted Shuso Imada of the Japan Sake and Shochu Makers Association. He told us that the Japanese National Tax Agency (NTA) chose not to impose minimums, so these rules act more as guidelines to help the consumer choose sake in the context of a brewery's lineup or regional trends. Although the NTA doesn't require breweries to state the sake type (e.g., junmai, honjozo, or daiginjo) or polishing ratio on their labels, most do so that consumers can make choices based on these figures. That said, there are brewers who don't put any such information on their labels. We consider these types of brewers to be punk rock and nonconformist, sending a message of, "Don't categorize me, just taste me!"

DON'T BOX ME IN!

A vertical rice-polishing machine.

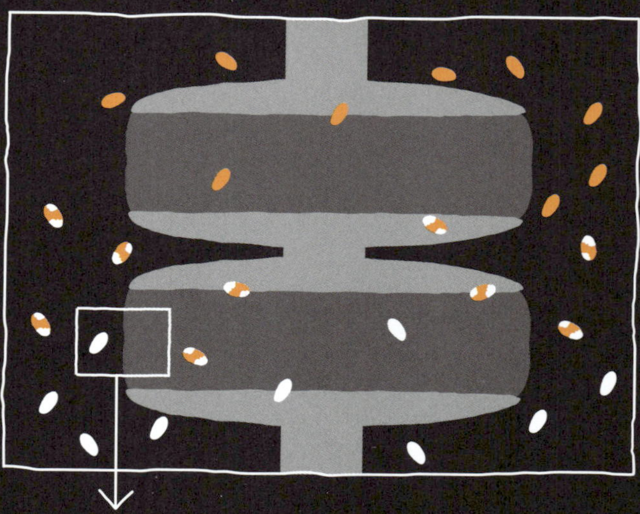

Stone wheel at bottom of machine.

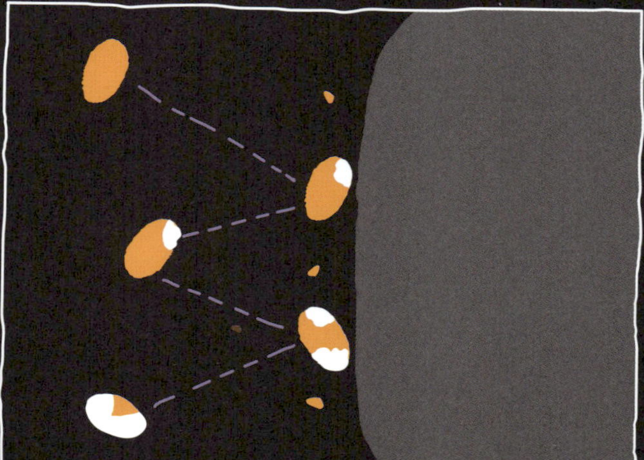

Close-up of the rice grains hitting the stone and the outer layer of the rice grains scraping off.

How Rice Is Polished

Vertical rice polishers, which were invented in the early 1900s, are used for milling rice. Brown rice (i.e., unprocessed rice) is fed into the top of the cone-like structure. Then, as the rice travels down the cone, it passes against stone grinders at the center of the cone that rotate and polish off the outer layer of the grains. (The powder that is polished away is sucked out from below and used for animal feed or confections.) The newly polished grains are then sent up the cone again, getting smaller with each pass until the desired rate of polish is achieved. Sake-makers slow down the speed of rotation as the rice grains get smaller and more brittle, thereby removing a thinner layer each time. It takes about eight hours to polish rice to 70% and about sixty hours to polish rice down to 10%.

Rice-polishing techniques have evolved greatly over the past few decades, and more brewers are now using rice that uses the flat-polished (*henpei*) technique. With conventional polishing rice is polished into a spherical shape, which is not true to the original oval shape of a rice grain. The result is that too much is shaved off the tops and bottoms of the grains and not enough from the sides. Flat polishing solves this issue by shaving off the outer layers of the rice equally from all sides, resulting in an oval grain that matches the contours of the original.

The result is that a sake made with 60% flat polished rice tastes like a sake made with 40% conventionally polished rice. This newer technique has challenged tokuteimeishoshu, the current system of basing sake types on rice-polishing ratios, and is a hot topic. Refer to Typicity of Sake: An Evolving History on page 34 for more.

Note: The term "rice polishing" is synonymous with "rice milling." We use these interchangeably in this book.

7 CLASSIC SAKE TYPES

Now we can marry the two factors (whether or not there's added alcohol and the amount of rice polishing) that affect how a sake type is determined, by looking at the seven types of sake we most commonly see. You'll have cracked the code once you've familiarized yourself with these types!

RICH + BOLD

CLEAN + AROMATIC

Rice polishing (maximum)	Type	Added alcohol	Flavors	Characteristics
100%	Futsushu	Yes	Alcohol, syrupy, sweet	Table grade, used for cooking and excluded from premium types because of an extra ingredient or high polishing ratio
100%	Junmai	No	Umami, savory, bold	Full-bodied, great warm; pair with meats, cheese, or rich foods
70%	Honjozo	Yes	Light, clean, umami, dry	Good everyday sake; pair with chicken, salmon, or fries
60%	Junmai ginjo	No	Fruity, complex, light	Great chilled; pair with chicken or shellfish
60%	Ginjo	Yes	Fruity, aromatic, clean	Great chilled; pair with salmon, tuna, or salad
50%	Junmai daiginjo	No	Floral, fruity, complex, refined	Great chilled, highly fragrant; good on its own or with raw fish or fruit
50%	Daiginjo	Yes	Floral, fruity, complex, aromatic, clean	Great chilled, elegant, highly fragrant; good on its own or with raw fish or fruit

COMMON CHARACTERISTICS

Flavors:
Cereal, sugary, alcohol

Finish:
Simple, short

Texture:
Velvety, light

TEMPERATURE SUGGESTION
Chilled
Room temperature
Warm

SERVEWARE SUGGESTION
Ceramic cup
Glass sake flute

OCCASION
Ball game
Dorm party

FOOD PAIRING
Fried food
Grilled meat
Pub food

OUR FAVES
Kirinzan Futsushu
Tozai Typhoon Futsushu

FUTSUSHU

Rice-Polishing Ratio (maximum): 100%

Ingredients: Rice, water, koji, yeast, distilled alcohol (up to 50% of the weight of the rice), additives, sweeteners, stabilizers

Translated as "ordinary sake," futsushu is considered an economical option of lower quality than the following six types of sake we discuss (think vin de table). There is no rice-polishing ratio regulation for this sake, and it has the most relaxed rules as far as adding distilled alcohol and additives.

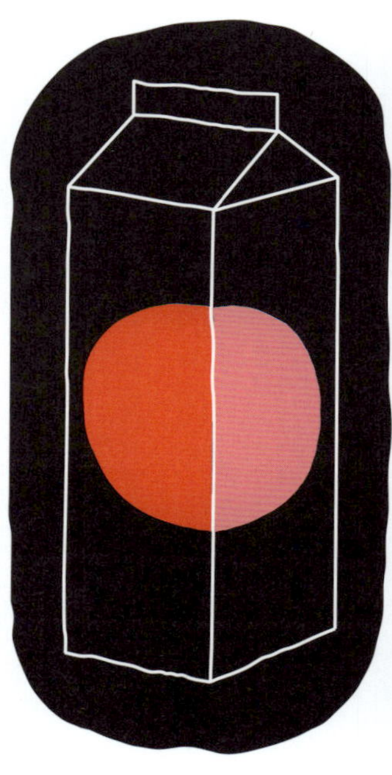

Demand for futsushu is falling in Japan as consumers are increasingly seeking quality over quantity. For that same reason, we rarely see futsushus here in the U.S. However, it still makes up about 60% of the entire Japanese sake market. It is also produced in mass quantities to be used as an ingredient in sauces and dressings.

Note: Sakes that would otherwise be considered premium may end up being labeled as futsushu if they fall outside the strict guidelines of premium sake. These include *kijoshu* (a type of sake that uses sake instead of water) and sakes aged in whisky barrels that may leach whisky back into the sake, thereby introducing a new ingredient.

JUNMAI

Rice-Polishing Ratio (maximum): 100%

Ingredients: Rice, water, koji, yeast

Junmais do not have a rice-polishing ratio minimum, and the one brown rice sake we tried with no added alcohol was considered a junmai. Typically junmais have a rice-polishing ratio of 70%, which still allows plenty of rich, earthy flavors to come through in the final brew.

Although not all junmais are alike, they tend to be full-bodied, rich, and bold. Since these sakes use rice that retains much of the outer layer of the grain, the flavor notes tend to include rice and grains.

These sakes are often robust, with savory aromas: nuts, mushrooms, dried fruit, and caramel. Due to their earthy flavors, these sakes are great at room temperature or served slightly warm in a wide-bowled wine glass or ceramic cup with a wide rim. A junmai may also have heightened acidity, which makes it a great sake to pair with heavier foods like red meats and savory cheeses.

COMMON CHARACTERISTICS

Flavors:
Umami, banana, nuts, bread, koji

Finish:
Medium dry to bold, full

Texture:
Rich, full-bodied

TEMPERATURE SUGGESTION
Room temperature
Warm

SERVEWARE SUGGESTION
Wide-bowled wine glass
Ceramic cup

OCCASION
Steak night
Thanksgiving

FOOD PAIRING
Cheese
Red meat
Mushrooms

OUR FAVES
Shinkame Junmai
Daishichi Junmai Classic
Umami Mart Junmai

HONJOZO

Rice-Polishing Ratio (maximum): 70%

Ingredients: Rice, water, koji, yeast, distilled alcohol (up to 10% of the weight of the rice)

The addition of distilled alcohol at the end of fermentation is intended to enhance the aroma of the brew, making honjozo less viscous and more silky—thus easier to drink. The addition of alcohol slightly increases the ABV immediately after pressing, but water is then added for dilution.

Honjozos have an image of being dry and easy to drink—a.k.a. sessionable. Not cloying or overly complex, honjozos are clean and affordable. Because they typically use rice with a higher polishing ratio, honjozos share some aromatic characteristics with junmais—think notes of bread, grains, and freshly steamed rice. However, because of the added alcohol, they tend to have a lighter texture and less rice-forward aroma than the junmais.

Try a honjozo in a sake flute, thoroughly chilled in a white wine glass, or slightly warmed in a ceramic cup. Because of their crisp, dry profile, honjozos are common in izakayas, and they pair well with bar foods like french fries, yakitori, onion rings, and burgers.

COMMON CHARACTERISTICS

Flavors:
Crisp, dry, bread

Finish:
Clean, short

Texture:
Light, velvety

TEMPERATURE SUGGESTION
Chilled
Room temperature
Warm

SERVEWARE SUGGESTION
Glass sake flute
White wine glass
Ceramic cup

OCCASION
Pub night
Weekday refresh

FOOD PAIRING
Roasted tomatoes
Salty snacks
Pork

OUR FAVES
Ichinokura Mukansa Extra-Dry Honjozo
Yuki Otoko Snow Yeti Honjozo

Tokubetsu Junmai and Honjozo

A brewer will usually make several types of sakes, from a junmai or honjozo to a daiginjo—covering the full spectrum of sake types discussed thus far. Oftentimes, nestled in the lineup will be a *tokubetsu*.

The tokubetsu—meaning "special" in Japanese—might be a souped-up version of their standard style. It may be either a sake that has a rice-polishing ratio of 60% or one made with a special brewing method. A brewer, for example, might have a junmai ginjo in their lineup made with rice polished to 60% and then release a tokubetsu junmai made with a special rice, also polished to 60% to highlight the rice. We have seen a good number of tokubetsu sakes offered in limited quantities for a short time.

PRO TIP: When you see one on a restaurant menu, take a chance on a tokubetsu junmai or tokubetsu honjozo. We are often pleased with tokubetsu styles when flying blind!

Why Are There No Tokubetsu Ginjos or Daiginjos?

Before the current sake rating system, which is called *tokuteimeishoshu* (started in 1990), there was a different grading system called *kyubetsuseido*. The earlier system was confusing because of its arbitrary standards. Government officials would determine which of three classes different sakes fell into: First, Second, or Top. While brewers often made sakes using rice polished to 70% in two classes, they rarely made sakes using rice polished to 60% in more than one class, simply due to the price point and lack of demand—see Typicity of Sake: An Evolving History on page 34 for more.

Shuso Imada of the Japan Sake and Shochu Makers Association speculated that this may have been because the market for sakes using highly polished rice was still nascent when the kyubetsuseido system was in place. When the tokuteimeishoshu system—which identifies sake types by rice-polishing guidelines—was established, the officials included the tokubetsu type to replace what would have been the Second or Top class for junmai or honjozo sakes. They did not create a tokubetsu type for ginjo or daiginjo, since few brewers made what would have been Second or Top class ginjo or daiginjo sake.

JUNMAI GINJO

Rice-Polishing Ratio (maximum): 60%

Ingredients: Rice, water, koji, yeast

The word *ginjo* means "carefully brewed." Junmai ginjo sakes use very highly polished rice and their aromas are of fruits and flowers, rather than rice and grains. Because only 60% of the grain remains in the rice used to produce these sakes, most of the proteins and fats are removed. This allows the flavor of the starchy core of the rice to reveal itself, no longer upstaged by the fuller flavors of those proteins and fats (as in a junmai or honjozo sake).

Another defining factor of junmai ginjos and ginjos (see opposite) is that they usually use specific ginjo yeasts. Yeast No. 9, procured from the Brewing Society of Japan, is commonly used in junmai ginjo and ginjo sakes; in addition to providing a stable environment for fermentation, it enhances fruity and floral fragrances.

Junmai ginjos are a great introduction to sake for beginners, as they are delicately sweet but still light and citrusy. When they are served chilled in a white wine glass or sake flute, the aromas—ranging from green apple and lemons to tropical fruit—shine. They are a fine choice for a picnic, seafood dinner, or vegetarian meal.

COMMON CHARACTERISTICS

Flavors:
Fruity, green apple, citrus, melon, banana

Finish:
Aromatic, subtly sweet, silky

Texture:
Refreshing, light

TEMPERATURE SUGGESTION
Chilled
Room temperature

SERVEWARE SUGGESTION
Glass sake flute
White wine glass

OCCASION
Picnic
Seafood dinner
Vegetarian feast

FOOD PAIRING
Fresh cheeses
Oysters
Poke
Salads and greens

OUR FAVES
Fukucho Moon on the Water Junmai Ginjo
Hakurakusei Junmai Ginjo
Akabu Junmai Ginjo

GINJO

Rice-Polishing Ratio (maximum): 60%

Ingredients: Rice, water, koji, yeast, distilled alcohol (up to 10% of the weight of the rice)

Most of the information related to junmai ginjos—including that on yeasts, aromatic characteristics, and serving suggestions—also applies to ginjos. But because ginjos incorporate more alcohol in the brewing process, their bouquet is further enhanced. The fruity flavors of green apples or lemons may linger a bit longer on the palate. Ginjos also have a more refreshing texture than junmai ginjos, making them a great aperitif. Summer is a great time to have a cold, crisp ginjo in a white wine glass or sake flute.

COMMON CHARACTERISTICS

Flavors:
Fresh fruit, melon, green apple, citrus, honeysuckle

Finish:
Aromatic, clean, silky

Texture:
Refreshing, light, dry

TEMPERATURE SUGGESTION
Chilled

SERVEWARE SUGGESTION
Glass sake flute
White wine glass

OCCASION
Brunch
Beach day
Vegetarian feast

FOOD PAIRING
Ceviche
Oysters
Fresh greens

OUR FAVES
Koshi no Kanbai Ginjo Tokusen
Yoshinogawa Gokujo Ginjo
Dewazakura Oka Cherry Bouquet Ginjo

JUNMAI DAIGINJO

Rice-Polishing Ratio (maximum): 50%

Ingredients: Rice, water, koji, yeast

The *dai* in *daiginjo* means "big," so we think of the translation for daiginjo as "extra carefully brewed." Removing at least half of the outer portion of the rice grains unlocks even more delicate aromas and flavors from the core of the grain. Along with these more floral characteristics, the texture of the resulting brew is close to that of water, as the fats and lipids from the outer layers of the rice grain are barely present.

One of the first things you will notice about a junmai daiginjo is the bouquet that engulfs you. Sake-makers deliberately brew daiginjos to "wow" the drinker with complex aromas. From marshmallow to strawberry blossoms and melon, junmai daiginjos can exhibit a range of flavors that might remind you of a fruit salad or a flower garden. In addition to the Yeast No. 9 used in making ginjo, producers of junmai daiginjos and daiginjos also often use Yeast No. 1801 to achieve these complex aromas.

Enjoy junmai daiginjos at room temperature or chilled in a red wine glass or tumbler. We like a glass with a wide mouth so we can stick our nose in to enjoy the scent of these sakes. The delicate nature of junmai daiginjos make them an ideal pairing for lighter foods like white fish sashimi or fresh tofu, or just for sipping on their own.

COMMON CHARACTERISTICS

Flavors:
Floral, ripe melon, strawberry, peach

Finish:
Long, complex

Texture:
Silky, can be light or rich

TEMPERATURE SUGGESTION
Chilled
Room temperature

SERVEWARE SUGGESTION
Tumbler with a wide mouth
Red wine glass

OCCASION
Wedding
Anniversary
Birthday
Promotions

FOOD PAIRING
Sashimi
Braised vegetables

OUR FAVES
Hanaabi Junmai Daiginjo
Houou Biden Asahi Mai Junmai Daiginjo
Nabeshima Aiyama Junmai Daiginjo

DAIGINJO

Rice-Polishing Ratio (maximum): 50%

Ingredients: Rice, water, koji, yeast, distilled alcohol (up to 10% of the weight of the rice)

Most of the information about junmai daiginjos—including that on yeasts, aromatic characteristics, and serving suggestions—also applies to daiginjos.

Daiginjos are the most common entries in the top sake competitions. Having a little boost of distilled alcohol highlights the bouquet and preserves the aroma in the bottle. The cleaner, silkier texture of daiginjos also leaves a better impression, especially when tasting sake without food.

If you are feeling super fancy, or want to spoil someone with a gift, a daiginjo sake will make a statement.

COMMON CHARACTERISTICS

Flavors:
Floral, ripe melon, strawberry, peach

Finish:
Fragrant, long, complex

Texture:
Silky, luxurious, airy

TEMPERATURE SUGGESTION
Chilled

SERVEWARE SUGGESTION
Tumbler with a wide mouth
Red wine glass

OCCASION
Wedding
Promotion
Anniversary
Birthday

FOOD PAIRING
Sashimi
Braised vegetables

OUR FAVES
Gasanryu Kisaragi Pliant Moon Daiginjo
Konteki Tears of Dawn Daiginjo
Kokuryu Crystal Dragon Daiginjo

SAKE STYLES

If sake types are like nouns, sake styles are the adjectives. Most styles of sake are created after the main fermentation. For example, a brewer who makes an umami-rich junmai may decide to skip dilution to make the umami even stronger. Or one who makes a fruity ginjo and wants to enhance its freshness may bottle it unpasteurized. But some styles develop earlier, when making the *moto* (fermentation starter).

Many of the styles we describe in the following section are related to our discussion about post fermentation on page 31. Brewers don't just bottle sake after it is fermented and kick off their shoes to watch cat videos on YouTube. There are many more decisions producers make before they deliver the final product.

Understanding how types and styles work together may take some time to grasp. But if you know the seven types of sake (see pages 42 to 53) and apply a style on top of it, you can begin to get an idea of how they work together.

In certain cases, the styles are just as important as the type when evaluating sake—some might even say they're more important. Look out for these key styles and how they affect the taste of the sake.

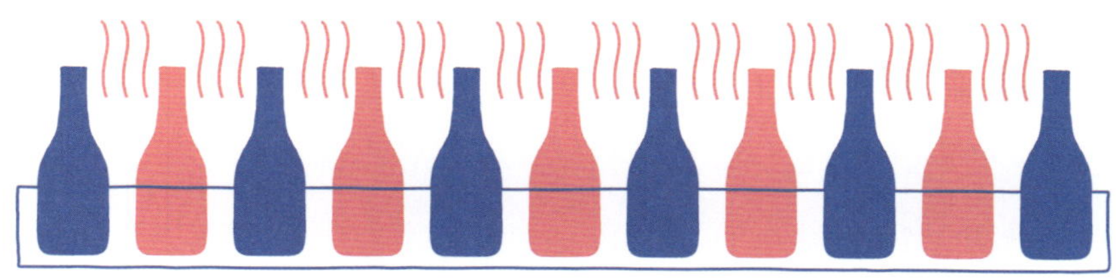

SAKE FINISHING STYLES AT A GLANCE

Style	How it's incorporated	Why it's applied	Characteristics	Tips
Nama	Skips one or both pasteurizations	To capture the just-brewed fresh flavors and textures of a sake	Yeast, sourdough, effervescent, alive, bold	Great to enjoy in the spring when many brewers tend to release namas
Nigori	Uses a coarse filter during pressing, allowing more *sake kasu* (sweet rice lees) to pass through	To give the sake a cloudy texture and sweeter flavor profile	Sweet rice, mochi, coconut, rice pudding	A sweeter profile opens possibilities for pairing with spicy food
Genshu	Skips water dilution after storage	To deliver a sake with a higher alcohol content or a more concentrated flavor	Longer finish, more alcohol flavor	Can be enjoyed on the rocks
Muroka	Skips charcoal filtration after pressing	To capture the natural qualities of the water and present a sake with a slightly yellow color	Weightier texture or heightened aroma	Serve in a clear glass to enjoy the color and viscosity as it grips the glass
Kimoto + yamahai	Lactic acid is allowed to develop naturally during the moto	To make a sake in the traditional style	Pronounced acid, yogurty, sturdy, mushroomy	Acidity pairs well with rich, fatty foods like meats, cheeses, and butter
Jukuseishu + koshu	Aged for longer than a few months (jukusei) or more than 3 years (koshu)	To develop rich caramel flavors and colors in the sake, especially if aged at room or outdoor temperatures	Caramel, sherry, dried apricots, mushrooms	Serve in a snifter as an after-dinner drink
Taruzake	Aged in cedar barrels for a few weeks	To impart minty and cedar flavors to the sake	Minty, herb, cedar	Delicious when served warm!
Sparkling	Either by adding CO_2 or using naturally occurring techniques (as for pétillant wines)	To give the sake a unique bubbly texture	Refreshing, sweet, bubbly	Good for brunch, outdoor events, and celebrations

COMMON CHARACTERISTICS

Flavors:
Fruity, yeasty

Finish:
Long, spicy

Texture:
Bold, effervescent

TEMPERATURE SUGGESTION
Chilled

SERVEWARE SUGGESTION
Glass sake flute
White wine glass

OCCASION
Friday night
Outdoor spring or summer party

FOOD PAIRING
Crudités
Raw oysters
Ham and prosciutto

OUR FAVES
Den Blue Label Nama Junmai
Kameizumi Eternal Spring Nama Junmai Ginjo
Sho Chiku Bai Nama Organic Junmai

NAMA

Unpasteurized Sake

The word *nama* means "raw," and here it refers to unpasteurized sake. You can read about why sakes undergo pasteurization in "Post Fermentation," page 31. Namas can skip one of the two pasteurizations or both. Look for an onslaught of nama sakes released in the early spring. This was traditionally the time when the brewing season came to a close and brewers would celebrate by releasing *shiboritate namas* (fresh-pressed sakes).

The following terms designate different versions of nama:

Nama or Namazake: General terms for all unpasteurized sakes, which are usually released in spring. You may also see the word *haru*, meaning spring, in the name to denote the season's release.

Namanama or Honnama: This type skips both pasteurizations.

Shiboritate: This sake usually skips both pasteurizations; it is bottled right after pressing in the winter and is one of the first releases of the brewing year.

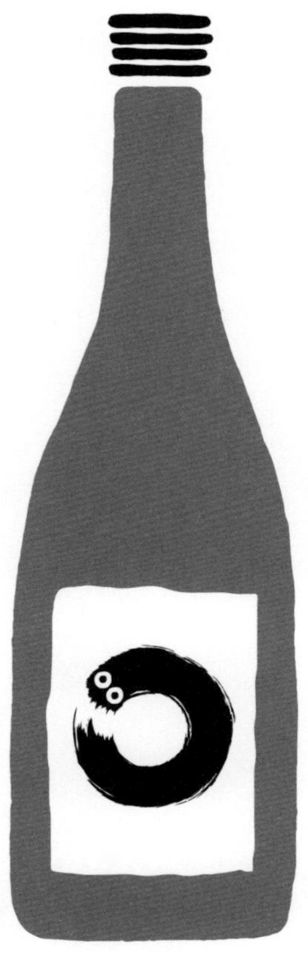

Namazume: Sakes pasteurized right after pressing and stored at a low temperature for about six months. These sakes skip pasteurization right before shipping.

Namachozo: Sake that skips pasteurization after pressing and is stored at a low temperature for about six months, then pasteurized right before shipping. Namachozos and namazumes enjoy the best of both worlds because they are "half" pasteurized. They may retain some of the lively flavors of a namanama (which skips both pasteurizations), but they are more shelf-stable because they have been pasteurized once.

PRO TIP: If you order a "nama" at a restaurant in Japan, they will invariably bring you an ice-cold beer on tap. Make sure to say "namazake" to get an unpasteurized sake!

SEASONAL NAMAS

In Japan, the practice of eating and drinking according to the changing seasons is embedded in the lifestyle. It's ice-cold, personal-size one-cup cans in the warmer seasons, and in winter, it's all about gathering friends and family around the *nabe* (hot pot) to share hot sake. You bet there are new releases of sake (usually namas!) to go with all the seasonal changes.

Spring

The birds are chirping and flower buds are sprouting! Spring is the optimal time to enjoy namas. Floral, fresh, and often effervescent, they are bold and best showcase sake as a fresh and vibrant beverage.

At Umami Mart, we host NamaFest every spring and pour all the namas available to us here in the States. We've seen the availability of these fresh spring brews multiply over the past few years, and our customers can't get enough of them! People come out for the raw, vibrant sakes to celebrate the sunny days ahead. If the cherry blossoms are blooming, it's a sign that namas are being released!

TRY THESE: Harada Arabashiri Nama Junmai Ginjo, Kagatobi Gokkan Junmai Muroka Nama, Takahiro Noble Arrow Tokubetsu Junmai Nama

Summer

Natsuzakes, or summer sakes, are typically released starting in June, and they satisfy thirsty sake lovers throughout the hottest months in Japan. Natsuzake is a pretty recent phenomenon, first appearing on shelves in the late aughts. Traditionally, there was a dip in sake sales during the summer, as there was no sake equivalent to an ice-cold beer or glass of sparkling wine—typically the drinks of choice for summer. Sake-makers knew that a summer sake needed to have similar attributes as these beverages: easy-drinking, low alcohol, light, fresh, and sparkling. To ensure that they can be enjoyed over a long period of time (say, at a picnic or BBQ), the sakes need to be easy to drink.

TRY THESE: Akabu Hisui Junmai Ginjo Sake, Ryusei Ryofu Junmai Ginjo Nama, Shichida Natsu Junmai

Autumn

Enjoy full-bodied, earthy *hiyaoroshi*, which are released in the fall. Hiyaoroshi are sakes that have been pasteurized once in the winter, then are aged through the summer, and are released in the fall without a second pasteurization. Brewers can skip the second pasteurization because by the fall, temperatures are cool enough that the sake will not spoil. Hiyaoroshi typically have fuller flavors, like cream, grains, spiced pears, or nuts—these sakes are perfect for your Thanksgiving Day spread!

Try these: Jozen Mizuno Gotoshi Junmai Ginjo Namazume Hiyaoroshi, Daitengu Usake Hiyaoroshi Junmai Ginjo, Jyoku Squirrel's Harvest Festival Junmai Genshu

World Sake Day

As all rice has been harvested by the end of September, October 1 marks World Sake Day, when breweries create new *sugidamas* (cedar balls), and hang them outside their buildings to denote the start of the brewing season. They may invite the local priest to bestow good luck on the brewery and its sakes for the coming year.

Traditionally, sake was brewed only during the winter, when the cold temperatures helped maintain the starter mash. As sake-making is now more automated and refrigeration makes it possible to brew year-round, we're lucky enough to get the freshest possible brews virtually all year long.

Winter

As sake-brewing season begins in October, there is a lot of sake released in the winter. These are the fresh, vibrant *shinshus* (meaning "new sake," usually made with the most recent rice harvest), *hatsushiboris* (first-pressed sakes that are released as the first batch of the season), and *shiboritates* (denoting "just-pressed," these are sakes that are shipped right after pressing in the winter). All three are usually not pasteurized; to preserve the just-pressed flavor and texture, we like to enjoy them chilled or at room temperature. These sakes typically have fresher, fruitier aromas that are often associated with ginjos and namas. We love these lighter flavors alongside oysters, crab, or a crudités plate.

In addition to these namas, taruzake (sakes aged in cedar barrels) is also released in the wintertime, as it is usually what is enjoyed on New Year's Day. Taruzake is delicious served warmed, which enhances the dryness from the cedar.

TRY THESE: Kid Junmai Ginjo Shiboritate Nama, Hito to Ki Junmai, Daisekkei Muroka Nama Genshu Tokubetsu Junmai

COMMON CHARACTERISTICS

Flavors:
Sweet rice, mochi, coconut, pudding

Finish:
Silky, rich

Texture:
Milky, effervescent

TEMPERATURE SUGGESTION
Chilled (shake gently to incorporate sake kasu)

SERVEWARE SUGGESTION
Glass sake flute
Ceramic cup

OCCASION
Korean BBQ
Brunch

FOOD PAIRING
Spicy meat or noodles
Dessert

OUR FAVES
Yuki no Tenshi Snow Angel Nigori Sake
Gozenshu Bodaimoto Nigori Junmai
Soma no Tengu Forest Spirit Junmai Ginjo Muroka Genshu Usunigori Sake

NIGORI

Coarsely Pressed Sake

Nigori means "cloudy" in Japanese, so it makes sense that a nigori sake looks like a wispy cloud when it is shaken. It is a style of sake that contains *sake kasu* (rice lees or solids) that have not fermented. You may hear nigori sake referred to as unfiltered sake, but a more accurate description is "coarsely pressed."

How does the kasu get into the sake? There are two main ways. One occurs during pressing, when a coarser mesh allows some of the kasu to pass through. The second way is to add kasu to a clear sake that has already been pressed. Back in the day (way back, in the 700s), sake was neither pressed nor filtered, as most sake was homemade and people were not in the habit of pressing and filtering it. These sakes looked similar to what we know as nigori sake today and were referred to as *doburoku* sake (see page 206). It was only well into the 1000s that both clear and unpressed sakes became abundant.

In the 1800s, the tax man came around and outlawed unpressed sakes to deter bootleggers, who wouldn't usually bother with elaborate pressing methods. In the 1960s, a Kyoto brewery called Tsukino Katsura released the first nigori. While it had the cloudy texture of unpressed sakes, it was still lawful since it was pressed, albeit through a coarser mesh.

With the current trend in Japan for lighter and drier nigoris, the range and quality of nigori sake is becoming vast and interesting. In fact, every time we go back to Japan, we see more and more *usunigori* sakes (lighter-style nigoris, mostly namas) appearing as limited offerings in department stores and on special menus at izakayas.

GENSHU

Undiluted Sake

COMMON CHARACTERISTICS

Flavors:
Boozy, sometimes fruity or bitter

Finish:
Long, bold

Texture:
Tingly, viscous

TEMPERATURE SUGGESTION
On the rocks
Chilled
Room temperature

SERVEWARE SUGGESTION
Glass sake flute
Ceramic cup
Rocks glass

OCCASION
Dinner party
Nightcap

FOOD PAIRING
Steak
Aged cheeses

OUR FAVES
Juemon Junmai Muroka Genshu
Tamagawa White Label Yamahai Muroka Nama Genshu Junmai
Wakatake Onikoroshi Tokubetsu Junmai Genshu

Genshus are undiluted or tank-strength sakes that are fresh, brash, and bold, best served on the rocks, in cocktails, or on their own. Sakes typically naturally ferment to 18 to 20% ABV, but you may have noticed that most are at 15 to 16%. To get down to 15%, brewers add water to the just-pressed sake. Adding a little bit of water can mellow out a sake and highlight its desirable flavors. Diluting also helps with lightening the viscosity. Genshus are often weightier and bolder than regular sakes.

If a sake has an ABV of 17% or higher, it's probably a genshu. But don't assume, in turn, that because a sake is at 15% ABV, it's not a genshu. Some brewers will deliberately stop fermentation early so that the sake reaches 15%. Why would they do this? They make a low-alcohol genshu to retain the bold flavors of a classic genshu but want to keep it at a low ABV.

Brewers often make a genshu in order to have a sake in their lineup that delivers a strong, flavorful punch. Genshus are often entered into sake competitions because they showcase the true, naturally fermented state of the sake. Since genshus are generally higher in alcohol, many sake lovers drink them on the rocks. Genshus are also a popular choice for our bartenders because of their ability to stand up to other ingredients due to their higher alcohol content.

Low-Alcohol or Nonalcoholic Sakes

While genshus satisfy drinkers who are looking for a sake with more body or a higher ABV, we've seen more low-alcohol options coming onto the scene as natsuzakes or nigoris, or simply as sakes labeled "low-alcohol." Look for sakes with ABVs of 14% or lower for these options. Additionally, sake lovers are turning to different ways to enjoy regular ABV sakes at a lower intensity, including in highballs (see page 182 for recipes), or just served on the rocks.

Amazake is a nonalcoholic sake that is made without yeast. It is sweet, thick, and full of umami. Every year, it is enjoyed by people of all ages around New Year's Day and Girl's Day in March, but we make it at home all year! There are some sake-makers who bottle amazake, but most of these sakes are highly perishable. Amazake is an excellent treat to bring to someone who is watching their alcohol consumption—or for the little ones in our lives!

Nonalcoholic sakes are on the rise in Japan, and there is also one made domestically here in the U.S. by Origami Sake. These alcohol-free alternatives, including amazake, are a healthy alternative to sugary drinks, while offering digestive benefits due to the active enzymes present.

COMMON CHARACTERISTICS

Flavors:
Savory, tart, earthy

Finish:
Long, bold

Texture:
Medium, weighty

TEMPERATURE SUGGESTION
Room temperature
Warm

SERVEWARE SUGGESTION
Ceramic cup
Wine glass

OCCASION
Dinner party
Holiday dinner

FOOD PAIRING
Turkey
Steak
Cheese

OUR FAVES
Shin Tsuchida Kimoto Junmai
Yuho Rhythm of the Centuries Yamahai Junmai
Matsunotsukasa Junmai Kimoto

KIMOTO + YAMAHAI

Traditional Fermentation Starter Techniques

Biodynamic, slow, and *natural*—these are buzzwords that are often used when talking about farming or wine. But how do we talk about those methods in terms of sake-making? We've always considered kimoto and yamahai sakes to embody these three characteristics. Capturing the power of living microorganisms, kimotos and yamahais are arduous, unpredictable, and Old World—making one is a true labor of love.

In the kimoto and yamahai methods, temperature control is key, as high temperatures can result in unwelcome bacteria, while low temperatures may inhibit the growth of lactic acid. It is a delicate balance that must be controlled through every hour of the day, and the results pay off in depth of flavor and aroma, thanks to a very wild and healthy yeast mash.

In the early 1900s, kimoto and yamahai were replaced by a simple brewing method called *sokujo.* Instead of taking advantage of naturally occurring lactic acid bacteria over time (as the kimoto and yamahai methods do), the sokujo method allows brewers to add industrial lactic acid to the starter mash—thus saving at least two weeks in sake-making time. The sokujo method is also easier to control, as industrial lactic acid is more stable and predictable. As of the mid-2020s, only about 10% of sakes produced are kimotos or yamahais, but kimotos and yamahais capture an earthy complexity that no sokujo sake can.

The difference between kimotos and yamahais is that kimotos are made with a technique called "pole-mashing," for which the brewers mix the mash with large wooden poles. The yamahai method skips

this step and the ferment is left to its own devices, with less intervention, so it's sometimes considered even more wild than kimoto. However, the common characteristics of both of these sakes tend to be similar, so we often refer to kimotos and yamahais together in this book.

The handful of brewers that still makes kimotos and yamahais are staunch believers in keeping these traditions alive. Inspired by old traditions, the Niida Honke brewery in Fukushima made a commitment in 1967 to return to its origins by using only organic rice, natural water, and ambient yeasts. The brewers at Daishichi Sake Brewery (considered the grandfather of kimoto brewing), also tried their hand at sokujo, but they eventually came to the conclusion that they could not brew the sake they wanted. The richness in taste they sought could not be achieved using the sokujo method, and as a result, today Daishichi brews only kimoto sakes.

Earthy, umami, and *nutty* are terms that come to mind when describing kimotos and yamahais. But we also love these sakes because they can be unexpected and interesting, cup after cup. And they are great food sakes, as their heightened acidity can stand up to heavier foods like cheeses and meats.

Minimal Intervention

Minimal intervention or natural sakes are those that are made with organic farming practices, use naturally occurring yeasts, highlight terroir, use traditional fermentation starters, and/or skip certain finishing styles.

On the additive front, sake is restricted by law to minimal intervention, since tokuteimeishoshu can be made from only five ingredients. The only additive sake-makers can use is commercial lactic acid, boosting the already naturally occurring lactic acid that forms during fermentation. Compare that to the sixty to seventy additives that wines can include without disclosure, and you get an idea of the purity of sake. No sulfites, chitosan, or Mega Purple allowed (e.g., juice concentrate or similar)!

Kimotos and yamahais are one way you can home in on your search for minimal intervention sakes. When we talked with Keizo Ishida of Matsuse Shuzo (Shiga), he explained that his kimoto sakes have no added lactic acid and use ambient yeast, so he can proudly proclaim they are additive-free. His other sakes, he said, contain only 0.4 liters of pure lactic acid and 0.2 liters of cultured yeast per 2,500 liters of sake. "In the wine world," he said, "all our sakes would be considered 'natural.' "

Another aspect you can look for that can be considered minimal intervention is in its style. Muroka nama genshus (or, as we lovingly refer to them, MNGs) are noncharcoal-filtered, unpasteurized, and undiluted sake. This means that MNG sakes express their characteristics right off the press. These sakes may have a certain color to them rather than being crystal clear, express some vibrant yeasty characteristics, and be higher in alcohol content.

Terada Honke (Saitama), Niida Honke (Fukushima), and Senkin Shuzo (Tochigi) are just three of the many makers known for brewing natural sakes as painstakingly as possible—using pesticide-free rice, traditional fermentation starters, and naturally occurring yeasts, and skipping some of the typical finishing techniques. Give these breweries a look if you are a lover of all things natty!

PRO TIP: Because sakes contain no preservatives, they are considered a fresh product and their shelf life is limited. As a rule of thumb, we tell customers to buy sake like you would beer, rather than wine (for more on storing sake, see page 198).

MUROKA

Noncharcoal-Filtered Sake

The word *muroka* means "not filtered," referring to sakes that have not gone through charcoal-filtering. You may be thinking, *Wait, I thought nigoris were unfiltered?* Although many people refer to nigoris as unfiltered, we prefer to describe them as coarsely pressed instead, since the term *nigori* refers to sakes that still contain some *sake kasu* (rice lees).

How do brewers use charcoal filtration, and why do they do it? After maturation, brewers typically mix powdered charcoal into the sake to absorb any impurities, remove rough flavors, and rid the liquid of any yellow tinge. Producing a clear sake is important for perception, as some people identify yellow sake as old sake. To show that the sake is not old, most brewers prefer to remove any color.

So why skip charcoal filtration? We asked a few brewers why they chose to go *muroka*. Some said they wanted to preserve the flavor of the water used, but most said they wanted a sake that has more *koku* (depth) and umami. Although this is a generalization, we have noticed that murokas tend to be mineral-forward, rugged, and viscous.

Charcoal-filtering is a relatively new process, developed around sixty years ago. As with any sake-making technique, using it or skipping it doesn't make a sake better or worse. Instead, it gives you insight into how the brewer made the sake and an opportunity to try a sake that is in a more raw form than other sake, most of which are charcoal-filtered.

COMMON CHARACTERISTICS

Flavors:
Minerally, earthy

Finish:
Long, rich

Texture:
Weighty and viscous, with slightly golden color

TEMPERATURE SUGGESTION
Chilled
Room temperature
Warm

SERVEWARE SUGGESTION
Glass sake flute
Ceramic cup
Wine glass

OCCASION
Tasting menu
Wine and cheese party

FOOD PAIRING
Caviar and oysters
Beans and nuts
Aged cheeses

OUR FAVES
Kuro Kabuto Muroka Junmai Daiginjo
Tae no Hana Sublime Beauty Arabashiri Kimoto Muroka Nama Genshu
Naraman Muroka Junmai

COMMON CHARACTERISTICS

Flavors:
Acidic, yogurty, grapeskin

Finish:
Long, sour

Texture:
Weighty

TEMPERATURE SUGGESTION
Room temperature
Warm

SERVEWARE SUGGESTION
Ceramic cup
Wine glass

OCCASION
Wine and cheese party
Grilling party

FOOD PAIRING
Cheese
Barbecue
Red chicken curry

OUR FAVES
Gozenshu Omachi Bodaimoto 1859 Junmai
Daigo no Shizuku Bodaimoto Nama Muroka Genshu Junmai

BODAIMOTO

Sake Made with an Ancient, High-Temperature Starter

We've been a bit obsessed with bodaimoto since we visited Shoryakuji Temple in Nara in 2023. Bodaimoto is a style of sake that uses a starter technique developed during the Kamakura (1185–1333) and Muromachi (1333–1573) periods. Shoryakuji's Head Priest Hironobu Ohara, who has been brewing sake there for thirty-eight years, explained to us that long before sake was brewed in the winter, it was brewed only during the summertime. Brewers had discovered that to prevent the fermentation from spoiling, they could create a starter with a highly acidic environment by combining water, uncooked rice, and just a little cooked rice. They would leave this mixture at ambient summer temperatures (which are very hot in Nara, around 80° to 90°F) to create *soyashi-mizu,* or sour water with lots of lactic acid. They would then separate the rice from the soyashi-mizu and save both. The rice would be steamed, and then the soyashi-mizu, cooked rice, and koji were combined for the starter. Traditionally, bodaimoto was made with *kuratsuki kobo,* or ambient yeast that lived in the brewery.

Bodaimoto is usually high in acidity (which makes it great for pairing with food) and exhibits a complex range of flavors (including banana, yogurt, mushroom, and sour grapes). We love surprising wine drinkers with bodaimoto—the acidity is familiar, but the umami flavors are a revelation. One of the coolest things about bodaimoto is that it allows you to step back in time, imagining that these sakes are pretty close to what people were drinking 800 years ago.

In the past, the word *bodaimoto* was used exclusively for sakes made with starter from Shoryakuji Temple. If the starter was made with the same method of using water and uncooked rice but did not come from the temple, you would refer to the sake as *mizumoto.*

JUKUSEISHU + KOSHU

Aged Sake

COMMON CHARACTERISTICS

Flavors:
Savory, umami, dried fruit

Finish:
Long, layered

Texture:
Velvety, viscous

TEMPERATURE SUGGESTION
Room temperature
Warm

SERVEWARE SUGGESTION
Ceramic cup
Wine glass

OCCASION
Holiday dinner
Nightcap

FOOD PAIRING
Steak
Grilled cauliflower
Desserts
Cheese

OUR FAVES
Kanbara Ancient Treasure Junmai
Tengumai Yamahai Junmai
Ichinokura Shozen Jukuseishu

Jukusei-shu is the general term for sakes that are aged for longer than the typical four months but less than three years. Their brewers are looking to mellow out acidity or bitterness, or simply to see how the sake progresses with additional time. Once the sake has matured to a desired profile, it is bottled and sold. But brewers aren't aging the sake to the point that it starts turning brown and exhibiting sherry-like characteristics.

Koshus are sakes that have been aged for a minimum of three years, typically at room temperature. They are a rarity, accounting for less than 0.1% of all sake produced. They are typically darker in color due to the Maillard reaction, which also makes them sweeter, fuller in umami, and with a fragrance reminiscent of sherry (see page 94 for more on the Maillard reaction). But don't let looks fool you—snow cave–aged koshus that are crystal clear have recently been released. These low-temperature aged sakes look like unaged sakes, but they taste complex and silky.

Sakes are too delicate to age in wood and are usually aged in stainless steel tanks or in glass bottles. The exception is taruzake (read on!).

TARUZAKE

Cedar-Aged Sake

During the Edo period (1603–1868), sake-makers began transporting their sakes in Japanese cedar casks called *taru* to reduce spoilage. They noticed that after long transportations, the wood imparted a minty fragrance to the sake that customers actually preferred.

With the distinct characteristics of Japanese cedar, or sugi—think minty, dry, peppery aromas—taruzake sake is not for everyone, as its fragrance can be overpowering. It's great, though, with very simple foods like edamame and vegetables, and best with salt, as they enjoyed it during the Edo Age.

With the advent of glass bottles and the ginjo styles of sake, taruzake has gradually declined in popularity over the decades because of its rustic qualities. However, taruzake is still believed to signify good luck and power and is often used for a *kagamiwari* (a barrel-breaking ceremony) at grand openings for businesses and during sumo championships.

Today, there has been a renaissance of taruzake, as various breweries experiment with techniques and uses of wood, from traditional to innovative. We also recommend warming up your taruzake.

COMMON CHARACTERISTICS

Flavors:
Minty, peppery, savory

Finish:
Short, dry, spicy

Texture:
Watery to syrupy

TEMPERATURE SUGGESTION
Room temperature
Warm

SERVEWARE SUGGESTION
Wooden cup or *masu*
Ceramic cup

OCCASION
New Year's Eve
Pub night

FOOD PAIRING
Fries
Chips and dip
Bonito

OUR FAVES
Yoshino Junmai Taru Sake
Hanatomoe Taru Maru Junmai

COMMON CHARACTERISTICS

Flavors:
Alive, sweet, fruity

Finish:
Medium

Texture:
Bubbly

TEMPERATURE SUGGESTION
Chilled

SERVEWARE SUGGESTION
Flute
Staight-sided glass

OCCASION
New Year's Eve
Brunch
Aperitifs

FOOD PAIRING
Raw oysters
Sushi
Burger

OUR FAVES
Masumi Origarami Sparkling Junmai Ginjo
Otokoyama Kita no Inaho Sparkling Sake
Chiyomusubi Sorah Sparkling Sake

SPARKLING

Naturally Sparkling or Force-Carbonated Sake

Sparkling sake has really only gained traction in the past decade or so. For many of its first iterations, the sakes were force-carbonated (CO_2 was added to the bottles). These sakes were usually very low in alcohol and sweet, which may have turned off serious sake drinkers. Since then, sparkling sake has evolved greatly. Brewers eventually began exploring methods for creating a natural sparkling sake, much like how pétillant naturel wines are produced. This turned out to be an incredibly difficult process for sake, and it has taken years of research and trial and error to get sparkling sake right for the market.

The main challenge is that nothing can be added to the sake to create the final, bubbly product or to adjust the sweetness. Although sugar can be added to Champagne, no distilled alcohol, acidifiers, or sweeteners can be added to make a sparkling sake. So you can appreciate how hard it would be to balance the sweetness and effervescence to produce an exquisite sparkling sake with fine bubbles without using additives.

The refinement and growth of this style of sake continues today. Unlike force-carbonated sakes, naturally sparkling sakes gain their bubbles when koji and yeast comingle with the residual sugars—thus producing CO_2. Sparkling sakes using the pétillant naturel method can be identified by reading the ingredients list on the label or by checking to see if the sake is included in the Japan Awasake Association list online.

Although Champagne has been the main influencer for sparkling sake production in Japan, sake has always had its own naturally occurring effervescence. Sakes like arabashiri, kassei nigori, and many freshly pressed namas all have a noticeable fizz, so sakes with bubbles are not at all a new concept. But today we are lucky enough to have a wide range of sophisticated, drier bubbly sakes for every occasion

TYPE + STYLE IN ACTION

Here are some examples of how sake types and styles work together. (Remember: Think of the types as nouns and the styles as adjectives.)

Muroka Nama Genshu Junmai Ginjo

If we have a junmai ginjo, we know it's going to have some fruity characteristics. Perhaps some green apple notes. And because it's a muroka nama genshu, the sake may have a yellow tinge, as well as some sourdough aromas and a higher alcohol content. We think this sake is going to be a punchy fruit basket with plenty of character!

Nigori Honjozo

This sake is coarsely filtered. So it's going to have some cloudiness to it and some sweetness. The fact that it's a honjozo tells us that there's an intent to give it a cleaner texture, perhaps balancing out the sweetness of the lees.

Koshu Junmai

Expect this sake, aged for more than three years, to have some rich honey notes and sherry-like characteristics. An umami-rich junmai may also have developed a savory, mushroom-like aroma due to aging.

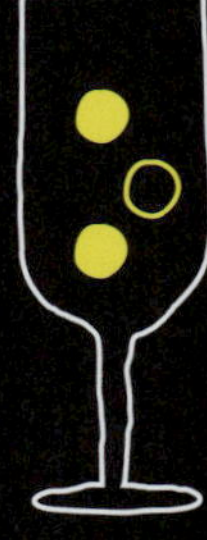

Sparkling Daiginjo

Bring out the Champagne flutes and ice bucket! This highly polished, refined sake is going to be fancy not only because it's a daiginjo, but also because it's got bubbles. We'd drink this before dinner or at a raw bar stocked with oysters and uni.

JAPAN'S EIGHT REGIONS

Japan is about 90% of the size of California but inhabits drastically different climates and terrain. From the northern tip of snowy Hokkaido to the southern tropical islands of Okinawa, Japan is divided into eight regions, and further subdivided into 47 prefectures.

Unique sake styles and flavors are found throughout Japan within these regions, since the local cuisine tends to mirror the available ingredients in the area. In this section, we highlight certain prefectures with characteristics for sake that are distinct in taste or brewing practices.

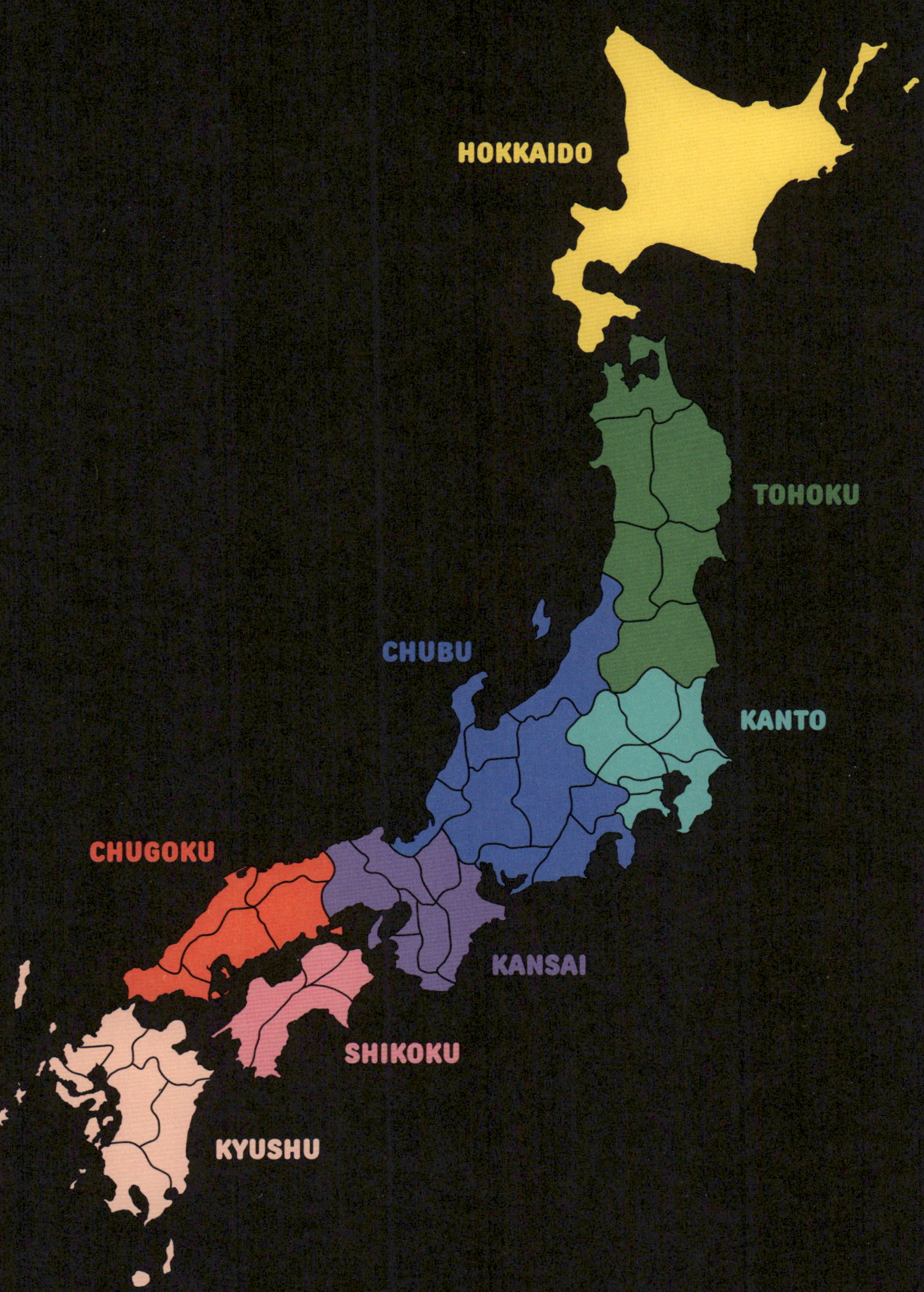
HOKKAIDO
TOHOKU
CHUBU
KANTO
CHUGOKU
KANSAI
SHIKOKU
KYUSHU

HOKKAIDO + TOHOKU

HOKKAIDO

SAKE PROFILE: Dry, rice-forward

LOCAL FOODS: Miso ramen and seafood, including crab, ikura, uni

FAMOUS BRANDS: Chitose Tsuru, Kamikawa Taisetsu, Otokoyama

Sake-making is newer in the coldest and northernmost island of Japan. Their brews are known to be dry and rustic to pair with more robust, regional flavors like lamb, uni, and miso ramen. Look for breweries using local Hokkaido sake rice, including Ginpu, which can result in rice-forward, creamy sakes that beg to be enjoyed warmed up.

FUKUSHIMA

SAKE PROFILE: Rich, soft, rice-forward

LOCAL FOODS: Shiso maki, ramen, gyoza

FAMOUS BRANDS: Daishichi, Homare, Okunomatsu, Kokken, Uka, Suehiro, Kinpou Yamahai, Naraman, Daitengu

Fukushima is home to countless award-winning breweries. The region has bounced back since the 2011 tsunami disaster, with its signature umami-forward sakes flowing, made by environmentally conscious brewers. The Kitakata area in Fukushima has a GI certification.

YAMAGATA

SAKE PROFILE: Fragrant, austere

LOCAL FOODS: Yonezawa beef, don-don yaki, konnyaku, fruit

FAMOUS BRANDS: Juyondai, Gasanryu, Ohyama, Dewazakura, Toko, Shuho, Takenotsuyu

Located in the Tohoku region, Yamagata is known for its hot springs and stunning mountain ranges. In 2016, Yamagata was the first prefecture to be awarded a GI in 2016.

AKITA

SAKE PROFILE: Viscous, fruity

LOCAL FOODS: Udon, iburigakko, kiritanpo

FAMOUS BRANDS: Akitabare, Ama No To, Aramasa, Dewatsuru, Taiheizan, Yuki No Bosha

Located in the north of mainland Honshu, this region is known for its picturesque, snowy winters. There, the Kodama Brewing Co. is famous for its technological advances in sake-making, including the Akita kimoto method. This development replaces the traditional kimoto method, which required brewers to separate the moto into small containers for hand mixing. Under the Akita method, brewers can now use an electric drill with paddles directly in the moto tank.

GEOGRAPHIC INDICATIONS: Since 2015, the terms *Japanese sake* and *nihonshu* have been designated as a Geographic Indication (GI). This helps ensure that the quality and reputation of Japanese sake is protected under the GI, as long as the sake adheres to strict guidelines pertaining to the use of local ingredients, brewing practices, and bottling.

More than twenty regions across Japan have GIs for their sakes, highlighting the unique locality of traits and helping to promote sake worldwide.

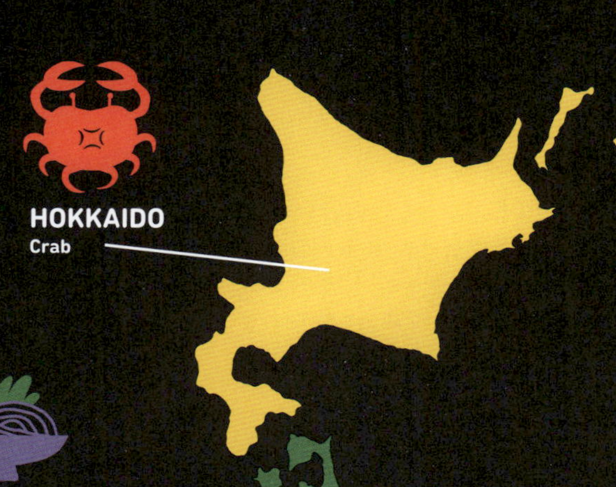

AKITA
Udon

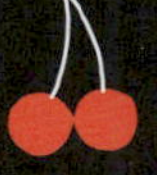

YAMAGATA
Cherries

FUKUSHIMA
Gyoza

CHUBU + KANTO

NIIGATA

SAKE PROFILE: Dry, crisp, clean

LOCAL FOODS: Hegi soba, "Italian" yakisoba, stir-fried ayu fish and noodles

FAMOUS BRANDS: Abe, Hakkaisan, Jozen, Kanbara, Kikusui, Kirinzan, Kubota, Midorikawa, Yuki Otoko

This prefecture is famous for its *tanrei karakuchi* style of sake, which is best translated as "dry, crisp, and pure." In February, Niigata sees more snowfall than Moscow or Montreal, and it is also home to the famous Sake no Jin festival, which celebrates sakes from around the country. Niigata sakes are often made using Gohyakumangoku rice, which results in lighter brews. The prefecture has a GI certification.

NAGANO

SAKE PROFILE: Crisp and refreshing to bold and hearty

LOCAL FOODS: Game (venison, duck, boar), soba

FAMOUS BRANDS: Daisekkei, Kisoji, Kizan, Masumi

This prefecture is known as the "Alps of Japan," with majestic mountain ranges and stunning landscapes. Tokyoites flock here during the summer for the cooler temperatures, while in the winter, Nagano becomes a prime destination for snow sports. The region's sakes are famous for using Miyama Nishiki rice, which generally results in crisp and refreshing sakes. The prefecture has a GI certification.

SAITAMA

SAKE PROFILE: Range of styles, from fruity to clean

LOCAL FOODS: Udon, miso potato, manju

FAMOUS BRANDS: Bunraku, Hanaabi, Chichibu Nishiki, Shinkame

Saitama is landlocked with neighboring Tokyo, so its perimeter is more of a commuter town for folks who work in the city. Go in a little deeper, however, and you'll find lush forests, wildflowers, and mountains. The region boasts pristine, mineral-rich water that's used for its renowned sakes and whiskies.

ISHIKAWA

SAKE PROFILE: Savory, dry, clear

LOCAL FOODS: Sushi, oden, lotus root

FAMOUS BRANDS: Kagatobi, Noguchi Naohiko Sake Institute, Tedorigawa

A convenient two-and-a-half-hour shinkansen ride from Tokyo, Kanazawa, the capital of Ishikawa Prefecture, offers a rich mix of history, culture, and delicious seafood. Often referred to as "Little Kyoto," here you can visit gardens and stores featuring local crafts by day and indulge in local delicacies by night, including isaki fish, gasu shrimp, and oden. To complement the local fare, sakes from Ishikawa are dry and clean (great for sushi) and savory (ideal for oden).

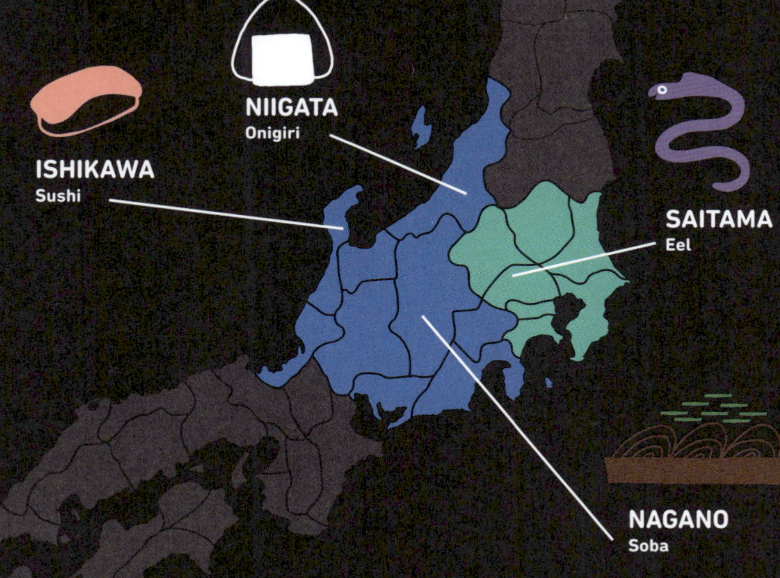
NIIGATA
Onigiri
ISHIKAWA
Sushi
SAITAMA
Eel
NAGANO
Soba

KANSAI

SHIGA

SAKE PROFILE: Steamed rice, dry finish

LOCAL FOODS: Ōmi beef, funazushi, red konnyaku

FAMOUS BRANDS: Daijiro, Emishiki, Kirakucho, Matsu No Tsukasa, Shichi Hon Yari

Home to the largest lake in the country, Biwa, Shiga is a landlocked region rich in pristine water from the lake and diverse soil types (with a long history of pottery making). The sakes of the region complement the rich local cuisine, especially the unique foods found in Biwa. Shiga was awarded a GI certification in 2022.

HYOGO

SAKE PROFILE: Rich, bold, sharp, dry

LOCAL FOODS: Kobe beef, akashiyaki, (octopus dumpling), sobameshi (stir-fried noodles and rice)

FAMOUS BRANDS: Fukuju, Hakutsuru, Kenbishi, Kikumasamune, Sawanotsuru

The birthplace of the mighty Yamada Nishiki sake rice, Hyogo is home to the Nada ward, or Nadagogo, the largest sake brewing area in Japan. Famous for its mineral-rich Miyamizu water, Nada's sakes are high in phosphorus, potassium, calcium, and salt yet low in iron, making it ideal for sake-making.

KYOTO

SAKE PROFILE: Soft, elegant

LOCAL FOODS: Tofu, pickles, sweets

FAMOUS BRANDS: Gekkeikan, Konteki, Takara, Tamagawa, Tama No Hikari

The Fushimi District in southern Kyoto is known for brewing sakes with its famous groundwater, which is rich in minerals. Kyoto's sakes are elegant, meant to pair with its upscale kaiseki.

NARA

SAKE PROFILE: Crisp, traditional, umami

LOCAL FOODS: Narazuke (pickles), somen, manju

FAMOUS BRANDS: Kaze No Mori, Choryo, Hanatomoe

We consider Nara as the epicenter for the beginning and future of sake, where modern techniques were created and perfected. Shoryakuji Temple in Nara is the birthplace of seishu, sandanjikomi, and bodaimoto. Brewers in Nara look to the area's past to learn about sake-making, while pioneering forward to create innovative brews.

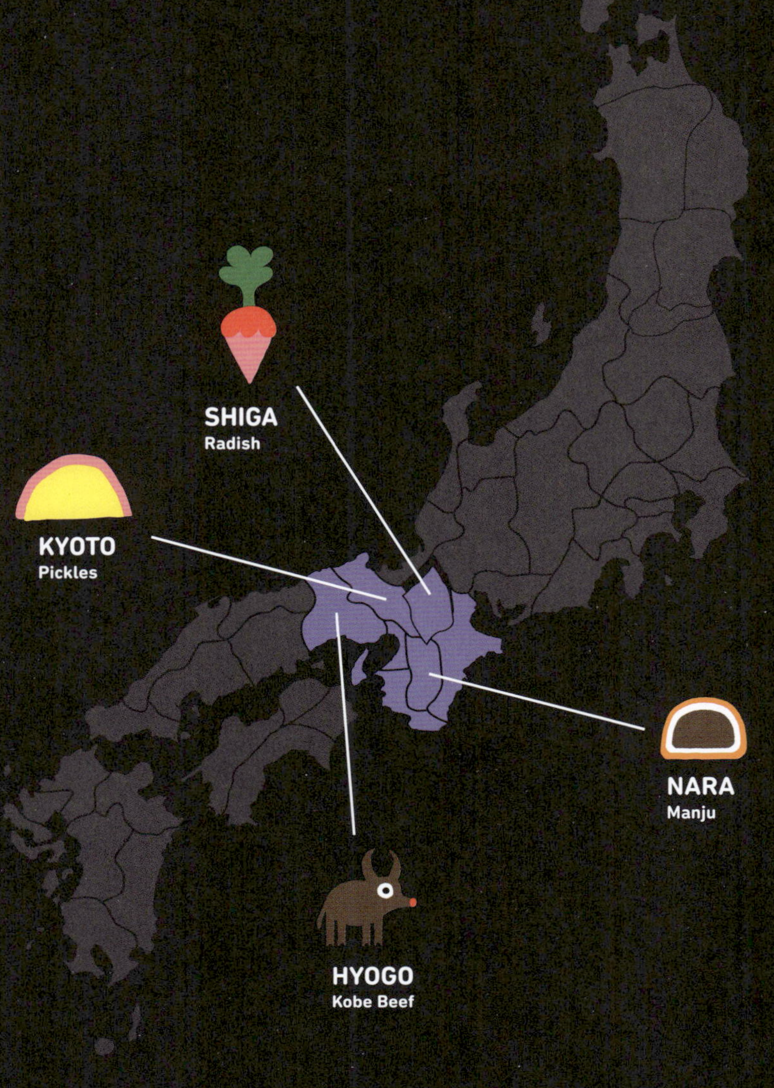
SHIGA
Radish
KYOTO
Pickles
NARA
Manju
HYOGO
Kobe Beef

CHUGOKU

HIROSHIMA

SAKE PROFILE: Fruity, tart

LOCAL FOODS: Okonomiyaki, oysters, anago

FAMOUS BRANDS: Fukucho, Hanahato, Kamoizumi, Kamotsuru, Sempuku

As the birthplace of ginjo sakes, this region is known for pioneering innovative sake-making techniques. The practice of using ginjo yeast and fermenting for longer at a lower temperature is credited to a Hiroshima brewer named Miura Senzaburō (1847–1908). Enjoy sakes with BGE (Big Ginjo Energy—see page 96) from this region.

TOTTORI

SAKE PROFILE: Bold, fruity, umami

LOCAL FOODS: Pear, Matsuba Crab, Tofu Chikuwa

FAMOUS BRANDS: Chiyomusubi, Mantensei, Inabatsuru

Home of Mizuki Shigeru, whose famous *GeGeGe no Kitarō* brought a cast of *yōkai* (supernatural creature or spirit) characters into the world after World War II, Tottori is a quiet prefecture that faces the Sea of Japan and is also known for their sand dunes (the location for the iconic 1964 film *Woman in the Dunes*). Not all is eerie in this sparsely visited prefecture, which we consider a gem of a destination. Enjoy seasonal matsuba crab in winter, juicy apple-pears in the summer, and sip on sake made with Goriki, a native rice to the prefecture. Tottori sakes made with Goriki tend to be bold, with ample fruit and umami.

YAMAGUCHI

SAKE PROFILE: Refreshing, light

LOCAL FOODS: Fugu, Iwakuni sushi, Sanzoku chicken

FAMOUS BRANDS: Dassai, Gangi, Gokyo, Harada, Ohmine, Taka, Tenbi

Situated on the furthest southwestern tip of Honshu before entering Kyushu, Yamaguchi is home to many prominent sakes including Dassai, known to brew junmai daiginjos exclusively. Sake from the Hagi area in Yamaguchi has a GI certification.

OKAYAMA

SAKE PROFILE: Deep, earthy, herbal

LOCAL FOODS: Eggplant, peach, muscat grapes

FAMOUS BRANDS: Gozenshu, Gokyo, Chikurin

When sake-lovers hear Okayama, they usually think of Omachi rice, the mother of all sake rice. Okayama is credited as the birthplace of Omachi and today grows most of it in Japan. While it's hard to grow this heirloom rice, with its tall stature and late harvest, sake made with Omachi is prized for its unique, earthy flavors and herbal aromas. Okayama Prefecture gets the most sunlight in all of Japan and, thus, has a long agricultural history. In addition to being a great place to grow rice, they are famous for growing fruits and herbs. Sounds a bit like California!

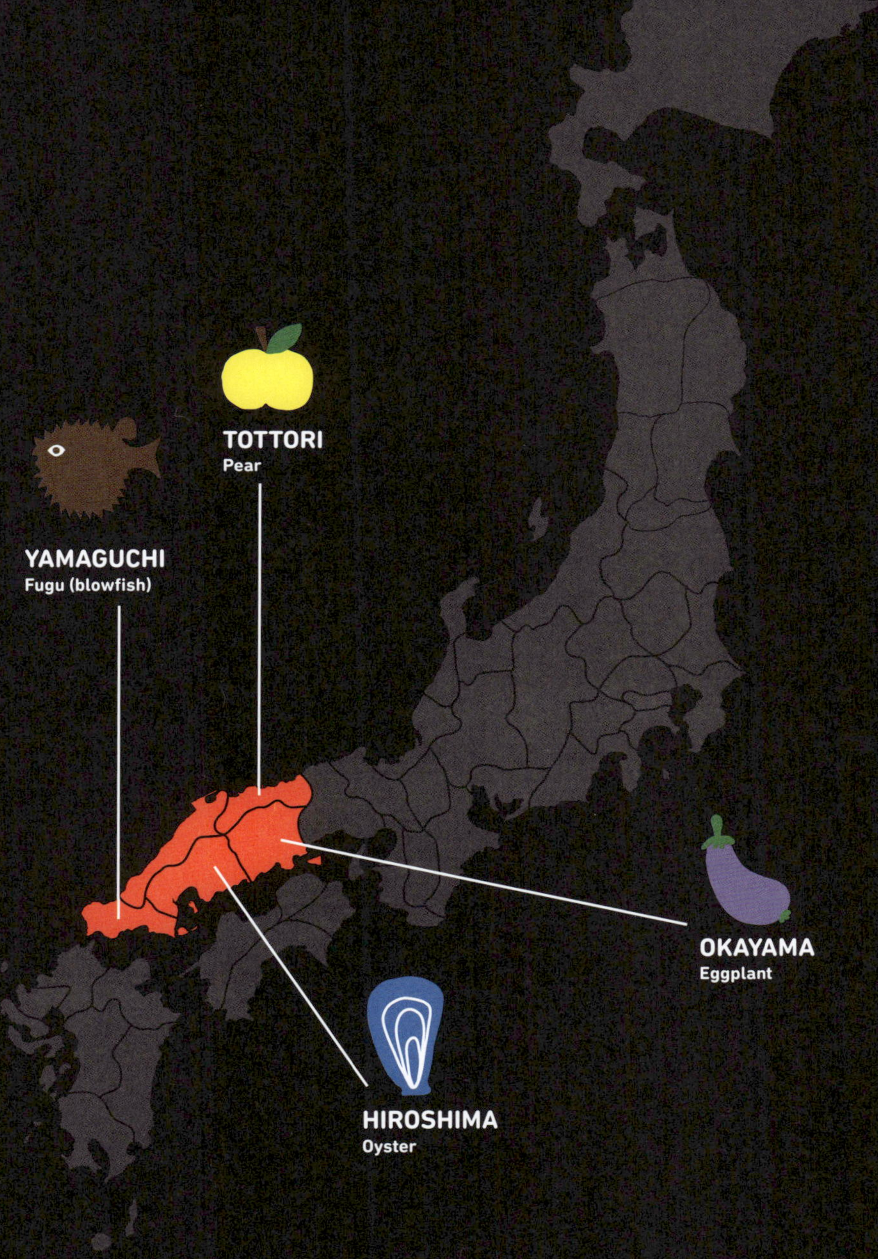
TOTTORI
Pear
YAMAGUCHI
Fugu (blowfish)
OKAYAMA
Eggplant
HIROSHIMA
Oyster

SHIKOKU + KYUSHU

KOCHI

SAKE PROFILE: Dry, or, more recently, very fruity

LOCAL FOODS: Bonito sashimi, udon

FAMOUS BRANDS: Bijoufu, Kameizumi, Suigei, Tosatsuru

This area has the highest per capita consumption of sake in Japan. Its sakes have long been well known as dry and easy to drink; more recently, on the opposite end of the spectrum, Kochi is also now known for its sakes made with the local Cel-24 yeast, bringing out fruity aromas like apples and mangoes.

TOKUSHIMA

SAKE PROFILE: Fruity, rich, clean

LOCAL FOODS: Grilled chicken, Dekonmawashi skewers, kaizoku ryori (pirate cuisine)

FAMOUS BRANDS: Narutotai, Housui

Located on the upper-eastern corner of the rugged island of Shikoku, Tokushima is famous for its mountains and rivers that weave in and out of the prefecture. Nature lovers will delight in hiking and rafting. Visit in August and partake in Tokushima City's Awa Odori festival, a spectacle involving thousands of dancers and over a million visitors. And while there, make sure to stop into Honke Matsuura, one of Japan's oldest sake breweries. Led by Motoko Matsuura, the brewery creates a range of sakes using exciting new techniques and ingredients, such as deploying a yeast developed in Tokushima using LED illumination.

FUKUOKA

SAKE PROFILE: Light, dry, refreshing

LOCAL FOODS: Hakata ramen, mentaiko, motsu

FAMOUS BRANDS: Kitaya, Kuro Kabuto, Niwa No Uguisu

Fukuoka has a diverse agricultural landscape with offerings such as their prized *gyokuro* (first-pick green tea) and a local strain of sake rice called Yume Ikkon, which is lauded for its low protein content. Sakes made with this rice are refined and light. There are more than 50 sake breweries in this region.

SAGA

SAKE PROFILE: Umami, velvety, robust

LOCAL FOODS: Saga beef, Yobuka ika, yudofu

FAMOUS BRANDS: Amabuki, Azumaichi, Koueigiku, Shichida, Nabeshima, Tenzan

Saga is famous for its thick soy sauce, beef, and squid, so their sakes must stand up to these strong flavors. As a result, the sakes are sturdy and bold, often with an assertive rice taste, a slight sweetness like cooked rice or mochi, and a robust umami flavor. Saga has a GI certification.

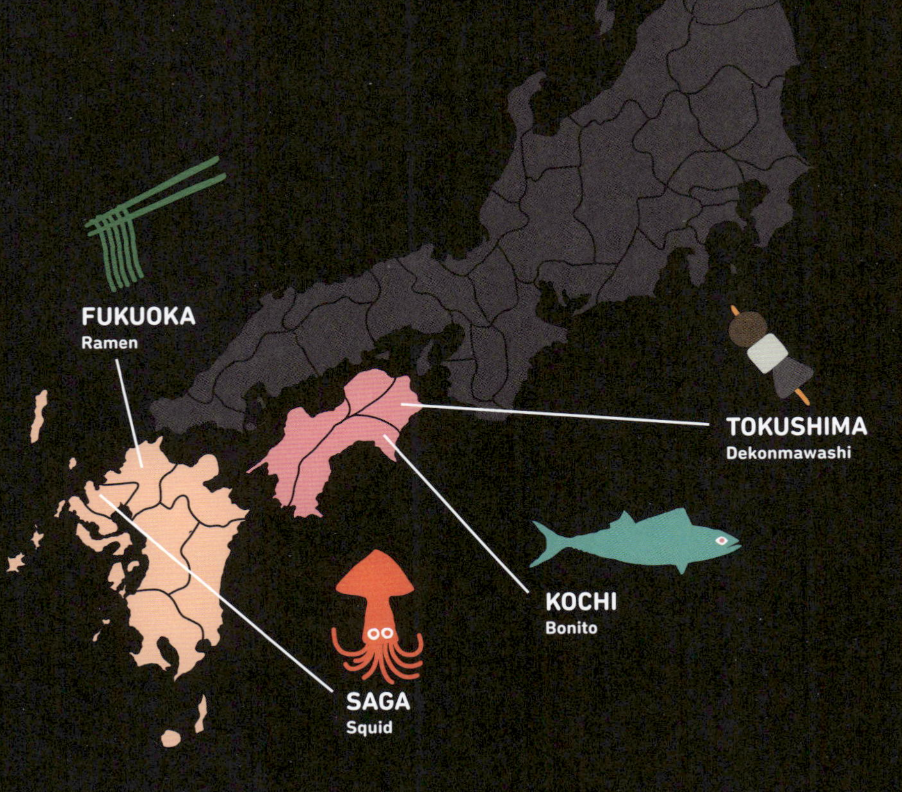
FUKUOKA
Ramen
TOKUSHIMA
Dekonmawashi
KOCHI
Bonito
SAGA
Squid

2

TASTE

Sweetness

Umami

Acidity

THE MAIN FLAVORS OF SAKE

The main flavors of sake are sweetness, umami, and acidity. Although sakes can have bitterness, it's not often at the forefront, as can be the case with beer. Sakes may also have some slight salinity, but quite rarely. Therefore, when identifying the main flavors in sake, it's most effective to concentrate on sweetness, umami, and acidity.

Sweetness

Sake most commonly express two types of sweetness.

The first one falls into fruity flavors like melon, apple, banana, and peach. These flavors are the easiest to identify on the nose and palate. They will hit you as soon as you lift the glass to your nose. These flavors are most common in ginjos and daiginjos. The word *ginjo* means "carefully brewed," and it refers to a style of sake that uses highly polished rice. Removing the outer layers of the rice grains means there are fewer amino acids and less protein content available as nutrients in the ferment. Because nutrients are low, fermentation temperatures are kept low to slow the release of nutrients and sugar as food for the yeast. If temperatures were higher, the yeast would use up the nutrients too quicky and fermentation would stop. Yeasts that are especially good at working at lower temperatures are often referred to as "ginjo yeasts." They include Yeast No. 9 and Yeast No. 1801. The low-and-slow starving of the yeast releases fruity esters (chemical compounds that result when alcohol bonds with organic acids and loses water molecules), thus revealing more fruity characteristics in the final sake. Desirable aromas for ginjos are apple, melon, ripe banana, pineapple, and cherry blossoms.

When you see the word *ginjo* or *daiginjo* on a label, think bright, fruity flavors and floral aromas. While there are always exceptions, this can be a starting point to your ginjo quest.

The second type of sweetness expresses notes of honey, caramel, and ripe banana. These aromas are often detectable in bolder junmais or sakes that have been aged and have undergone the Maillard reaction, a chemical reaction in which carbohydrates (sugars) and amino acids (proteins) are exposed to higher temperatures over time. You may be familiar with this reaction when you toast bread or sear meats.

With sake that's been aged at a higher temperature (or room temperature in all seasons), this chemical reaction is encouraged, and it results in an amber-colored sake. Sakes that have undergone this reaction can have roasted, malted, and umami flavors.

TRY IT!

Try these foods side by side to compare their levels of umami.

	Low in umami	High in umami
Cheese	Fresh mozzarella	Parmesan
Fruit	Apples	Tomatoes
Meat	Steamed chicken breasts	Dry-aged beef
Mushrooms	White button mushrooms	Shiitake
Sake	Daiginjo	Junmai (with a high rice-polishing ratio) or all-koji sake

Umami

While it's easy to identify a flavor as *sweet,* it can be more challenging to actually taste *umami.* Umami flavor is best described as savory or meaty and is most often associated with foods high in amino acids or peptides—think meats, broths (especially dashi), mushrooms, and cheeses. For the less scientifically minded, umami is the indescribably complex flavor that just makes you go, "Mmmm!"

So why is sake so high in amino acids despite not containing any meat or broth? The secret is koji. Koji mold spores are grown on the rice, and that is what makes sake both possible and unique among alcoholic beverages. Essentially, koji takes the place of the malting process that happens in beer. Koji creates enzymes that convert starch and proteins in the rice to sugars and amino acids that yeast can use for alcohol production. While koji performs a vital role during fermentation, it also contributes to the final taste of the sake. Brewers can control how the koji ultimately expresses itself in the sake. Sakes that have higher amounts of koji growth, such as junmais and honjozos, can have pronounced flavors of rice, umami, or nuttiness.

Too much umami, especially in sakes that haven't aged, can make the sake taste bitter or unpleasantly weighty. As with all aspects of sake, brewers are keen to control umami from the process of making koji to finding the sweet spot for aging. Yoshihiro Sako of Den Sake Brewery in Oakland believes that aging can smooth out the bitter edges of a freshly pressed sake and turn it into something more complex, like the tannins in wine.

Grain-forward flavors like steamed rice, toasted rice, barley, breakfast cereal, porridge, malt, yeast, and mochi are common umami flavors in sake. Sakes with higher rice-polishing ratios (meaning they use more of the rice grain), like honjozos and junmais, often exhibit these umami flavors.

Earthy and nutty flavors, including mushrooms, soy sauce, miso, and chestnuts, are also associated with umami in sake. **Look for sakes that use higher amounts of koji or more thoroughly inoculated souhaze koji, like junmais, honjozos, kimotos, and yamahais.** Although it is rare, we've seen some sakes that are labeled "all koji," meaning that all the rice used in production was inoculated with koji. These are certainly umami bombs with high levels of amino acids, and they almost taste like dashi!

Does Your Sake Have BGE (Big Ginjo Energy)?

One of our staff members was a huge acronym fan, and his most memorable creation was BGE, for Big Ginjo Energy. Whenever we embark on a sake tasting, we ask ourselves, "Does this sake have BGE (Big Ginjo Energy) or SJU (Super Junmai Umami)?"

If the sake has aromas of bright fruit or floral aromas, it may have BGE—think crisp ginjos with muscat flavors, or a junmai daiginjo bursting with aromas of melon and honeysuckle.

Or Does Your Sake Have SJU (Super Junmai Umami)?

Sakes that smell like steamed rice or pudding are more likely expressing SJU, and they are typically fuller-bodied junmais, kimotos, or yamahais. Try two sakes side by side and see if you can identify them as having either BGE or SJU.

Acidity

When we taste tart or sour flavors and our mouths water, it means we detect acidity. Highly acidic ingredients and foods include lemons, sauerkraut, and vinaigrette. Is your mouth watering yet? Although sake is much less acidic than wine, the acidity in sake still plays a big part, as it balances out sweetness. Acidity in sake mostly comes from the lactic acid that naturally occurs or is added during fermentation. Dairy flavors like yogurt and cream cheese from lactic and other organic acids that build up over time can contribute to acidity in sakes like bodaimotos, kimotos, and yamahais (the starters for these sakes take much longer to establish than sokujo, the most common starter method).

When tasting for acidity in sake, citrus flavors like lemon, lime, and tropical fruit that make your mouth water are also worth noting. Sakes exhibiting citrus flavors can include junmai ginjos and ginjos, as well as some sakes made with white koji (as opposed to the default yellow koji typically used in sake-making).

TRY IT! Try a light- to medium-bodied crisp Pinot Noir alongside a honjozo sake—honjozos tend to be on the light, crisp side of the sake spectrum. Notice the acidity. Does one of these make your lips pucker or your mouth water more?

Other Flavors

Not all sakes obviously exhibit sweetness, umami, or acidity—some have flavors that are outliers. A taruzake that has been aged in cedar barrels for a few weeks, for example, will have herbal, earthy flavors. Aged sakes may have flavors of fall fruits such as persimmons that are astringent. And genshus can have a pronounced alcohol flavor that tends toward bitterness, since these sakes have not been diluted with water. These flavors, although less common, are worth noting.

HOW TO TASTE SAKE

Now that we've familiarized ourselves with some of the main flavors in sake, we can start tasting. When tasting sake, your main objectives should be to ***identify, document, and summarize its characteristics.***

Before you taste, consider the following:

Vessel

We recommend tasting in a clear glass like a wine glass or a tumbler with a wide mouth. A clear glass will allow you to see the color and opacity of the sake, while the wide rim will allow you to get your nose in there so you can take in all the aromas.

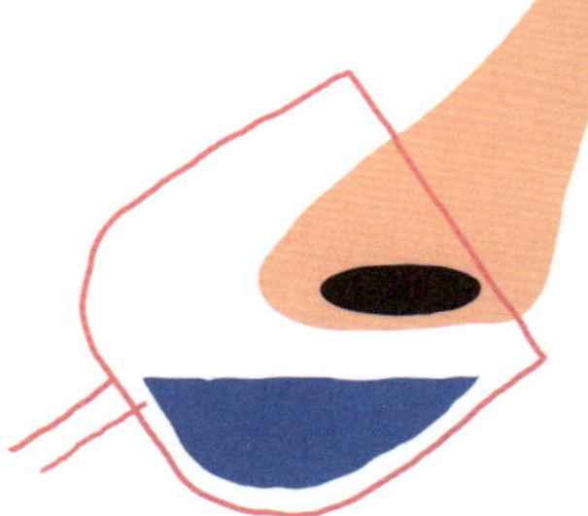

Temperature

We prefer tasting sakes at room temperature. We often find that detecting aromas in sakes right out of the fridge is a little tricky, as they are more difficult to pin down. If the sake is a touch too cold, warm the glass in your hands to bring up the temperature of the sake.

Light

Make sure to taste sake in a well-lit room, preferably with natural light. It is helpful to place a sheet of white paper underneath your glasses to assess the color and clarity as well. You can tell a lot about a sake even before lifting the glass off the table.

Palate

Be sure not to have any other flavors in your mouth before tasting. Tasting sake after a cup of coffee or mapo tofu for lunch doesn't work!

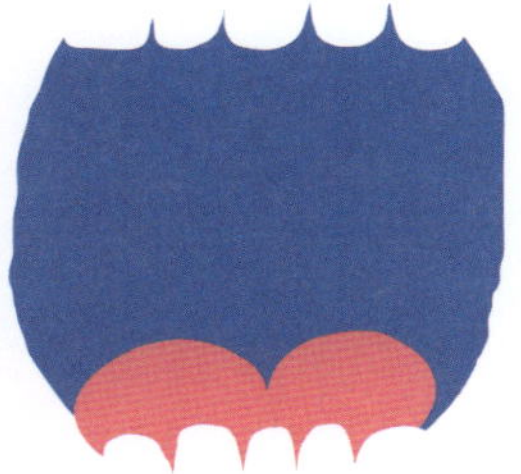

Side by side

We like to taste at least two sakes side by side for comparison. That way you can go back and forth and perhaps notice new things about them each time.

STOP DROP + ROLL

To identify the aromas and flavors in sake, it's good to have a vocabulary to describe its common characteristics and set parameters. Use our **Stop, Drop + Roll Method.**

Step 1: STOP and Look

There is a lot to notice when you stop and look at a sake before you taste it. Is it watery or translucent? Is it clear or amber? Although the appearance of sake might initially not be as obvious as that of white wine versus red, sakes can indeed look very different from glass to glass. The following are the characteristics to take note of before you even lift your glass off the table.

Opacity (Transparent to Cloudy)

If a sake is cloudy, it is likely that it is a nigori. This type has some sake kasu or rice lees still present because of the coarser filter used during pressing or because some of the sake kasu was added back to a clear sake. More cloudiness usually means that the sake will be sweeter, because sake kasu is sweet. The opacity of a sake can range from crystal clear to hazy or porridge-like.

Color (Clear to Yellow, Gold, Amber, and Brown)

The color of your sake depends on two key factors: charcoal filtration and aging.

Most sakes go through charcoal filtration, which removes unwanted odors and colors (sakes that do not undergo charcoal filtration are labeled as muroka). Pale yellow or lime colors may come from the koji.

Most sakes are aged after fermentation. How long a sake is aged and at what temperature can affect the hue.

Sake is generally aged in stainless steel tanks for about four months after pressing. Why a few months? Very fresh sakes can sometimes be too lively (with noticeable spiciness on the tongue) or taste bitter.

Use the terms in this word kit to take notes on the appearance of sake.

SAKE APPEARANCE WORD KIT

Ever feel like you just don't have the words to express yourself? That's where our word kits come into play. Refer to our word kits throughout this tasting section for the tools to describe what you are experiencing.

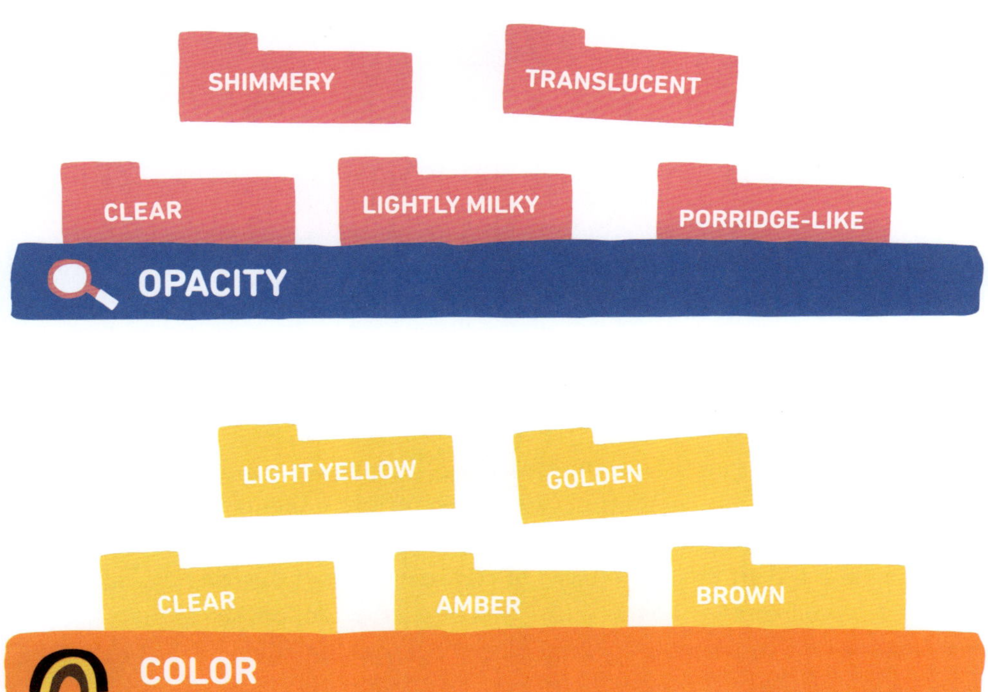

Step 2: DROP Your Nose Into the Glass

You can tell a lot from the aroma of a sake—in fact, we usually get most of our notes from simply sniffing. Most sake aromas fall into just three categories: fruit, grain, and dairy. When tasting sake, we like to ask ourselves, **"Is this sake a fruit basket, a bowl of rice, or a yogurt parfait?"** In most cases, a sake aroma will reveal itself as one (or more) of these.

When taking in aromas, try changing the variables involved. For example, start with the glass far away from you, then bring it in close. Harold McGee (author of several books on the science of cooking, including *On Food and Cooking*) suggests taking in long deep breaths then short pulses with your mouth open and then closed. "Vary how it gets to you in the brain, so your brain doesn't fall into a temporary habit," he says. "You end up getting different molecules into different parts of your nose. Pause occasionally for a minute or two, to let your sensors and brain rest and recalibrate."

At what point do you start detecting the scent of the sake? How does the aroma change when you breathe in and out? Do you detect new aromas in a sake after smelling something different, like pepper, and then coming back to it?

SAKE AROMAS WORD KIT

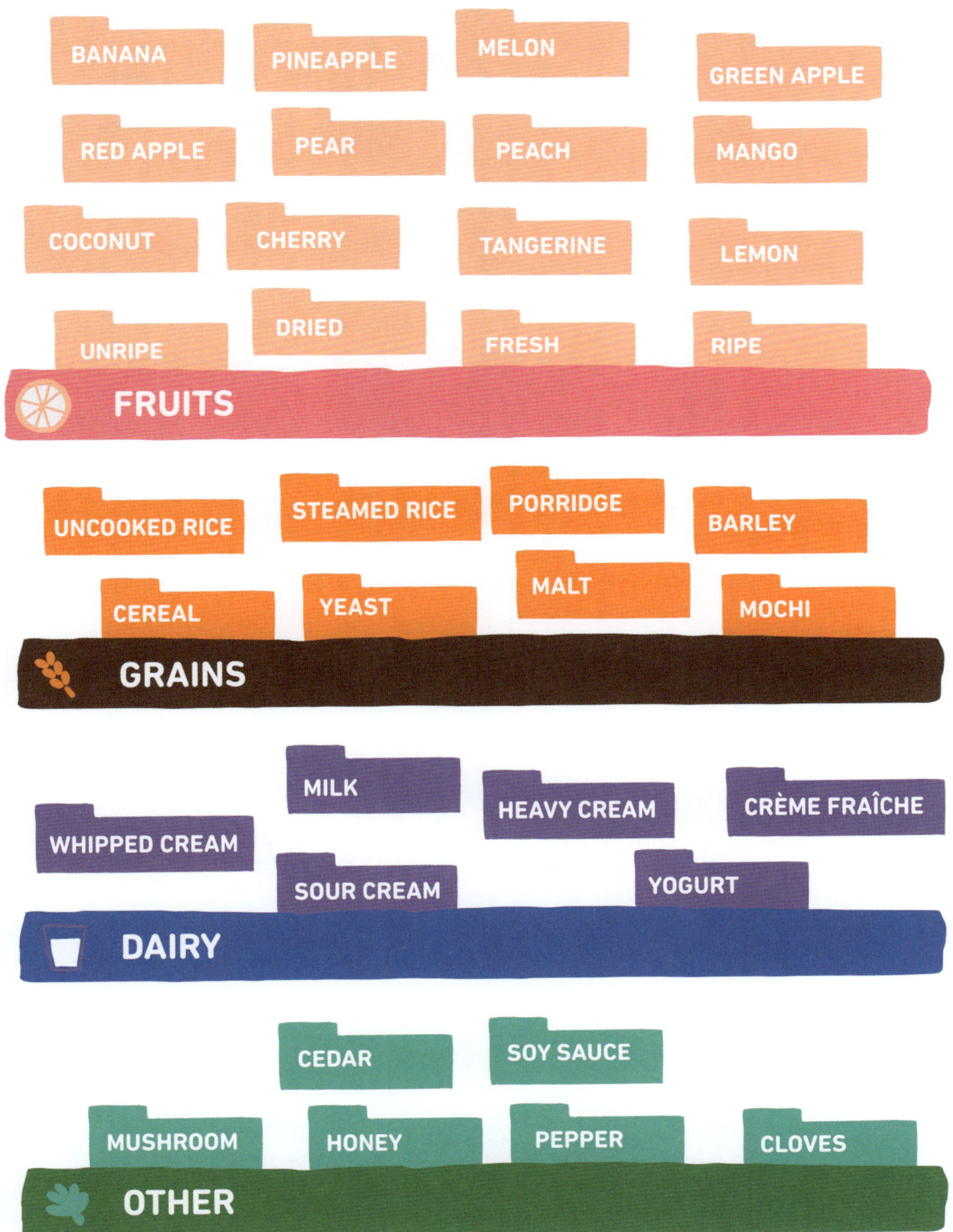

Step 3: ROLL It Around in Your Mouth to Taste

Sweetness

Sometimes it's hard to detect dryness in sake when other tastes like acidity are at play. Try to identify if you are tasting sweet flavors like candy or fruit juice. Or is the sake dry, with a "grippy" sensation in your mouth and no sugary flavors?

Umami

When tasting for umami, notice flavors associated with rice, grains, nuts, mushrooms, and miso. Fruity ginjos may have less umami, while savory junmais with age will be bursting with umami.

Acidity

If your mouth waters or your lips pucker when you are drinking sake, you are detecting acidity. While sakes are generally low in acidity compared to wine, kimotos and yamahai usually have higher levels of acidity that are worth noting.

Short to Long Finish

Short and long finishes are desirable in different contexts for sake. Niigata is famous for its clean, dry tanrei karakuchi sakes, while Hyogo's style boasts rich, bold finishes. A sake with good *kire* has a pleasantly quick and clean finish. A crisp, cold Japanese beer is often prized for its kire. To detect finish, we find it helpful to try at least two different sakes for the opportunity to compare and contrast.

SAKE FLAVORS WORDKIT

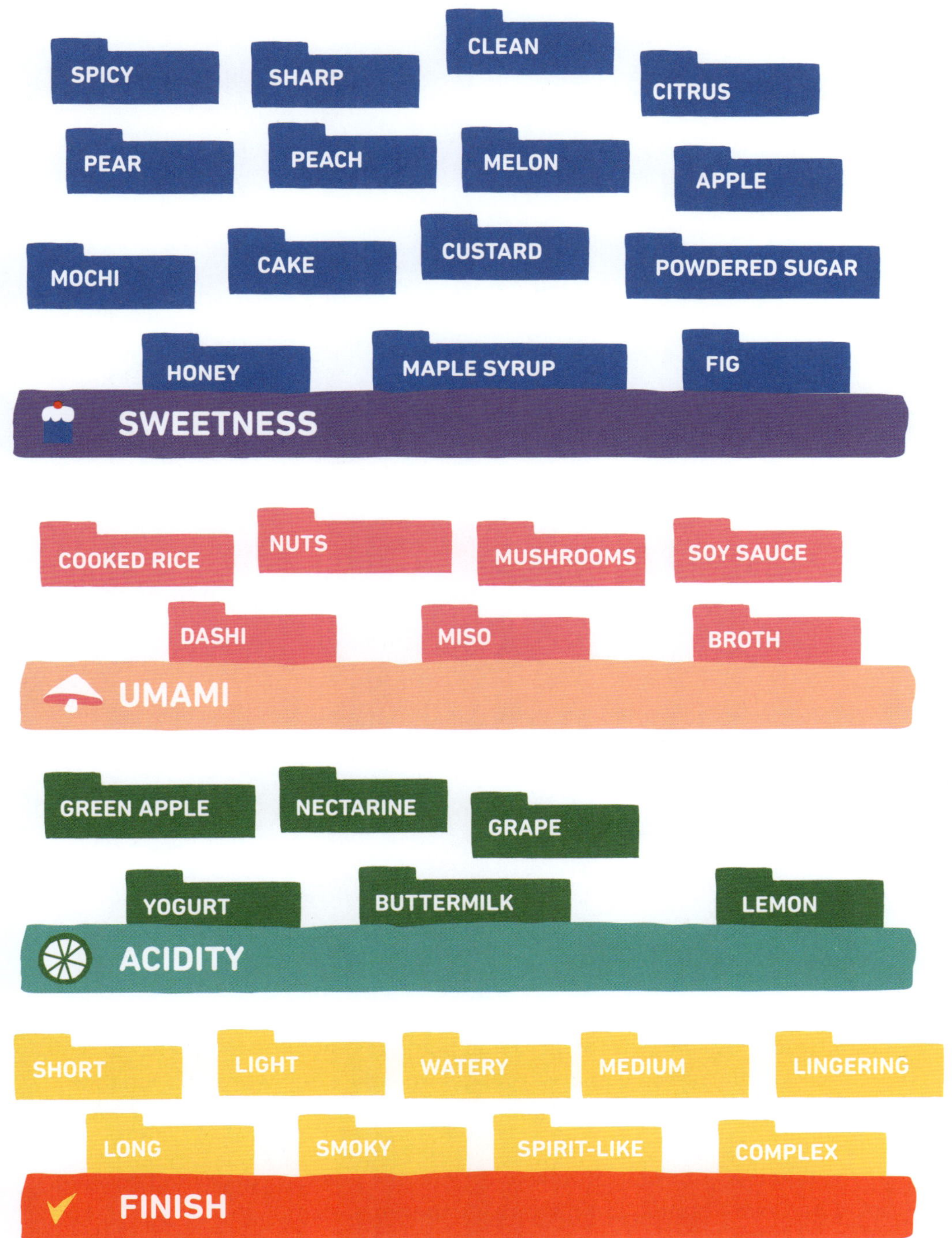

TRY IT!

How long does the drink's taste linger at the back of your tongue?

	Short	Long
Beer	Crisp pilsner	Chocolate stout
Wine	Vinho verde	Cabernet Sauvignon
Spirit	Vodka	Scotch
Sake	Honjozo	Junmai daiginjo genshu

Extra Credit! Go to our website to find blank tasting note templates and fill them out for the sakes you are tasting. Circle different words as you take in a sake's aroma and flavor. Add any additional characteristics that you notice.

You'll find an example of how to do it on the opposite page, and you can download more tasting templates at umamimart.com.

Date of Tasting	August 3, 2025	
Sake Name	Hanaabi Junmai Daiginjo	
Type/Style	Junmai Daiginjo	
Brewery	Nanyo Jozo	
Region/ Country	Saitama, Japan	
Look	Opacity	Clear | Shimmery | Lightly milky | Translucent | Porridge-like
	Color	Clear | Light yellow | Golden | Amber | Brown
Aroma	Fruit	Banana | Pineapple | Melon | Green apple | Red apple | Pear | Peach | Mango | Coconut | Cherry | Tangerine | Lemon Ripe | Unripe Dried | Fresh
	Grain	Uncooked rice | Steamed rice | Rice porridge | Pudding | Barley | Breakfast cereal | Yeast | Malt
	Dairy	Whipped cream | Milk | Heavy cream | Crème fraîche | Sour cream | Yogurt
	Other	Cedar | Soy sauce | Mushroom | Honey | Pepper | Cloves ____________________
Taste	Sweetness	Spicy | Sharp | Clean like water | Citrus | Pear | Peach | Melon | Apple | Mochi | Cake | Custard | Powdered sugar | Honey | Maple syrup | Figs
	Umami	Cooked rice | Nuts | Mushrooms | Soy sauce | Dashi | Miso | Broth
	Acidity	Green apple | Nectarine | Muscat grape | Red grape | Fresh cheese | Yogurt | Lemon | Lime
	Finish	Short | Light | Watery | Medium | Lingering | Long | Smoky | Spirit-like | Complex
	Other	BGE, fresh, silky
General Rating	From disliked to loved it!	1 | 2 | 3 | 4 | 5

In Summary

Now that we've identified the characteristics of the sake being tasted, it's time to put it together in your own words.

Based on the sample tasting sheet on page 111, the taster would say:

This sake is crystal clear. It's a fruit basket with BGE! I can smell aromas of melon and peach. It seemed dry to me overall, with a lingering finish and no rice-forward umami. Did I like it? Yes, I liked the silky ending, but the nose was a bit overwhelming with serious BGE.

If Mr. Fox tasted something that contrasted completely with the one described on the tasting sheet, he might summarize it by saying:

This sake is transparent but golden. We've got a dairy queen! But wait, I also feel like it's a rice bowl with SJU. The tart yogurty aromas hit me first in the nose, but I also get undertones of porridge and savory mushroom. I'm tasting a lot of umami, with some brothy notes and dried figs—must be high in amino acids. The yogurt-like acidity is also coming through on the long finish. This was an intense sake that I'd love to revisit with a rich meal like a steak, because I feel like it has the acidity and complexity to stand up to it.

TRY IT! Do this with at least two sakes, and you'll start to notice patterns. Practice tasting and you'll be talking about sake like a pro in no time!

HOW TO BUILD A SAKE FLIGHT

We build flights for customers every day at the bar so they can try a variety of flavors across three different sakes. For a typical flight, we choose sakes that represent our trusty analogies: a fruit basket, a bowl of rice, and a yogurt parfait! Serving a flight at a dinner party might at first feel intimidating, but if you use the same methods we employ for our flights, it's easy—serve the first as an aperitif, the second with the appetizer, and the third for the main course or dessert.

Flight component	Associated types and styles	Typical tastes and aromas	Pairing
1. Fruit basket: fruity, delicate, light	Ginjo, junmai ginjo, daiginjo, junmai daiginjo, sparkling sake	Melon, banana, cherry, apple, citrus	A light, fruitier style best served chilled in a wine glass alongside the apps to kick off the night
2. Bowl of rice: grain, rice, umami, bold, earthy	Junmai, honjozo	Rice, pudding, grain, cereal, mushroom, lactic acid	A medium-bodied sake that balances umami and acidity to accompany fried appetizers or the main course
3. Yogurt parfait: tart, umami, rich, custard	Kimoto, yamahai, koshu	Yogurt, red grapes, sherry, dried fruit	A full-bodied sake with higher acidity and sweetness to accompany rich main courses and desserts

CHOOSE

10 RULES FOR CHOOSING SAKE LIKE A SOMM (AKA KIKIZAKESHI)

1. LOOK FOR THE FRESHEST SEASONAL SAKE.

Sake brewers release sakes when they think the timing is optimal. This is especially true for young *namas,* or unpasteurized sakes. It takes about six months for sakes to arrive in the U.S. from Japan, and many brewers will account for this lag. They bottle their U.S.-bound sakes slightly younger than the sakes they intend to release in Japan.

When choosing sake, go in with the mindset of a shopper at a farmers' market rather than a Costco. In the springtime, fresh, seasonal, unpasteurized sakes appear, exhibiting vibrant, fruity flavors that are as fleeting as the cherry blossoms that bloom in Japan at around the same time. These sakes are often labeled as *shiboritate* or *namas*.

When summer comes around, sake-makers often release lower-ABV *natsuzakes* (summer sakes) that are crisp and best enjoyed ice-cold. They may also release higher-ABV *genshus* (undiluted sakes) that are great on ice.

As the rice harvest comes to a close and chestnuts start to appear in the fall, it's the season for *hiyaoroshi*—sakes that are pressed in the spring, aged throughout the summer, and released as soon as the weather cools down. These sakes are best paired with foods like oily fish, braised meats, and nuts.

On the production side, winter is prime time. Makers take advantage of sake yeasts that thrive at low temperatures and express a wide range of aromas and flavors. Look for flagship brews with fresh bottle dates. Winter is also a great time to enjoy fuller-bodied, umami-forward types like junmais and honjozos that you can serve warm.

While not all sakes have their bottle date stamped on them, many do. Turn the bottle around to see if you can spot a stamp that resembles YY/MM. We try to stock sake that was bottled within the past year and count ourselves lucky if shipments arrive within six months of the bottle date.

If you are at a shop or restaurant, ask them if they have any sakes that are seasonal, have a recent bottle date, and/or fit the current food landscape. It's a great way to celebrate each season.

  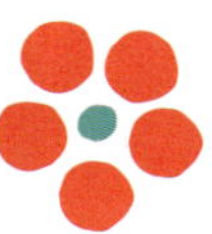 

2. EXPLORE BEYOND THE BIG FOUR SAKE COMPANIES.

There are currently about 1,500 sake breweries in Japan, and about a dozen of them are gigantic. Just as with beer, the biggest sake brewers account for most of the market share. Ozeki, Gekkeikan, Takara, and Hakutsuru all have their time and place, just like Coors, Budweiser, and Heineken. In fact, all of these national brands started small, and they continue to provide a gateway to microbreweries to survive through research. But when delving deeper into sake, try looking beyond these household names.

Sake microbreweries, though many times more numerous, are virtually unknown compared to the giants (especially in the U.S.). But because they are not catering to the mass market, many smaller breweries will go out on a limb to make a sake unique or specific to their region.

For example, a smaller brewery in Hiroshima may brew sakes that are specifically meant to be paired with oysters, a delicacy in that region. Or a family run, 400-year-old brewery in Gunma Prefecture may stick to the old ways, using only ambient yeast in its sakes. Makers who do not need to make huge yields to satisfy a large market have the freedom to create sakes that are distinctive or experimental.

So how can you distinguish sakes that are not made by the big companies? Try turning the bottle over and check out the name of the maker. Or ask your server or a bottle shop clerk if they have something from a smaller brewery.

Beyond not recognizing the brewer's name on the label, you can determine if a sake is made by a smaller brewer by considering the following factors: Is it made in a small city that you don't recognize? Does the description mention local rice, yeast strains, or water sources? Does the importer also bring in artisanal wines and beers? Does the bottle look and feel mass-produced?

Try something small! You may be rewarded with big flavors!

3. TRY A GLASS OR BOTTLE THAT IS ONE STEP UP FROM THE CHEAPEST ONE.

If your intention is to explore the world of sake, try anything above the cheapest option. While the budget bottle probably uses lower-grade ingredients or automated techniques or comes from a bigger brand, the slightly more expensive bottles are more likely to use better ingredients or handmade brewing methods, or come from a smaller brewer.

That said, there are always exceptions to the rule, as we do offer some great lower-priced options. If budget is key, ask the server or staff person for their opinion on the lower-priced items.

4. THINK OF GINJOS AS THE GOLDILOCKS OF SAKE.

When Goldilocks broke into the home of the three bears, she came upon three bowls of porridge. The first was too cold, the second was too hot, and the third, just right. We think of ginjo as the "just right" sake.

That's because ginjos and junmai ginjos please people who are new to sake and may be put off by a more rustic, umami profile, even in a sake delivering complexity in aroma and flavor. Ginjos are known to have pleasant, fruity aromatics, and their light to medium body works well with a range of food.

We've also found that people at parties enjoy having something chilled, giving ginjo more points as a crowd-pleasing sake. It is also not the most expensive bottle on the block (read on to our next rule for that), making it an ideal choice for gatherings.

5. TOAST WITH A DAIGINJO OR SPARKLING SAKE.

If it's a special occasion and you are seated at an omakase or Michelin-rated restaurant to celebrate an anniversary, birthday, or promotion, splurge on a daiginjo or a sparkling sake (see page 74).

Junmai daiginjos and daiginjos are brewed for opulent aromas, with highly polished rice and specific yeasts that can be floral in the nose. Sakes with these elegant aromas are best enjoyed in a big-bowled wine glass and with lighter foods like white fish or steamed vegetables, or as an aperitif. We like to start off a special occasion with a daiginjo before indulging in richer foods that may affect the palate.

Try a sparkling sake (especially one made in the pét-nat style) for a toast! Like Champagne, these sakes are excellent with oysters and other shellfish appetizers.

6. DIG INTO THE MAIN COURSE WITH A JUNMAI OR HONJOZO.

Junmais and honjozos both use rice that hasn't been highly polished and are generally fermented at higher temperatures than ginjos and daiginjos, making them fuller-bodied and umami-forward with higher acidity. Their bolder flavor profile allows more flexibility as far as food pairings go—especially for heavier main courses that feature meat, rich seafood, or cheese. And because junmais and honjozos aren't highly aromatic, they won't get in the way of the food.

Junmais and honjozos are also easier on the wallet than ginjos and daiginjos, making them great options for a style to sip all night.

7. SIP ON SOMETHING SWEET WHEN GOING SPICY.

Nigoris, or coarsely filtered sakes, are cloudy in appearance thanks to the *sakekasu,* or lees, that remain in the brew. The lees are sweet and have a creamy texture. Nigoris are often described as milky and dessert-like, and they can have hints of coconut, mango, and other tropical fruits.

We like to recommend nigoris to folks who don't like the bitter taste of alcohol, and we also find they are a great option for pairing with spicy foods. Their creaminess helps tamp down the heat. We love pairing nigoris with spicy foods like Lao papaya salad, Thai basil chicken, and Indian curries.

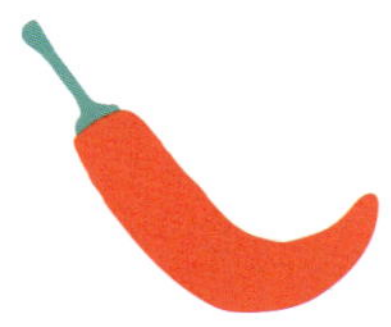

8. FINISH THE MEAL WITH AN AGED SAKE.

Most aged sakes have an amber hue, with notes of dried fall fruits and honey. They taste very different from your clear, garden-variety junmai or ginjo, offering a finish that can be long and complex—similar to a brandy or whisky. While they aren't aged like whisky in wooden casks, they do undergo a long aging process at room or cellar temperature that transforms them into a golden liquid with complex flavors reminiscent of sherry.

Enjoy an aged sake in a brandy snifter or heavy-bottomed rocks glass as an accompaniment to dessert or on its own as a nightcap. A wide-mouthed glass will bring out its complex aromatics and flavors of apricots, caramel, warm spices, and honey.

9. GO RUSTIC OR ARTISANAL WITH KIMOTOS AND YAMAHAIS.

If you are looking for something handmade and earthy, like your favorite locally made fresh goat cheese or churned Amish butter, try a kimoto or yamahai. These styles represent only about 10% of the total volume of sakes made. That is because they are very labor-intensive and take way more time to make.

So why do brewers still make them? They offer some very interesting flavors thanks to a traditional starter method that yields higher acidity and gamier notes. This less-controlled method can mean that these styles of sake can vary from year to year, allowing sake connoisseurs to look forward to each new release.

While kimotos and yamahais can be off-putting to daiginjo lovers, they are dreamboat styles for people who want to experience rustic, tart, and earthy flavors.

10. CHOOSE BY LABEL.

Brewers spend a lot of time and energy on the way they label their sakes. While you may not be able to read what's on the label, its color and shape are likely trying to tell you something. Is the bottle a cool blue, with a label that uses a wispy font? It may be telling you that this is a refreshing sake that's clean and fruity. Are there gold accents, with the neck of the bottle adorned in a ribbon? You might be looking at an elegant, floral daiginjo. Is the bottle brown, with traditional-looking *kanji* (Japanese characters)? This one might be a junmai or honjozo that is cozy and great when warmed. If you are really in a bind because there is no text on the label and the server or proprietor of the shop cannot give you any information, try to gather hints through the graphics and packaging.

We've noticed lots of more modern labels with clean graphics that stand out from labels with lots of kanji on them. These may mean that the brewer is, for example, dialing up the acidity or sweetness, or dialing down the alcohol, and signaling to the buyer that a sake is not going to taste like one you've had before. We often choose sakes because we like the design of the labels. Are you a dog lover, and the bottle has an illustration of a puppy on it? Is there a retro emblem that captures your inner graphic designer? If the brewer's visual style captures you, it's worth a try!

SAKE

LET'S ORDER SAKE!

Selecting Sakes at Bars and Restaurants

From a special-occasion celebration to a casual night out with the family, it can be intimidating to decide which sake to order. But talking to the server is not so different from talking to us at our shop—conversation is key to getting exactly what you want, so don't be shy! Feel free to ask lots of questions and be honest about what you like or don't care for. Whether you're sake-curious or a seasoned pro, you're sure to get some good nuggets when you talk to someone at the establishment about their recommendations. We've compiled some helpful hints to make it a breeze to order sake at a restaurant.

Start with the Words You Recognize

You might just need a few words to get the conversation with your server started so you can get the right glass for your mood (see Sake Mood Ring, page 148). Do you want something refreshing or complex? Do you want something fruity or earthy? Do you want something served chilled or warm? If you are a more seasoned sake drinker, try using words like *nama* (fresh and raw), *kimoto* (acidic), or *ginjo* (floral), which can help your server home in on your dream glass with more precision. Recognizing a region or prefecture you have an affinity for can also help you when choosing sake (see page 78).

Talk to the Bartender or Server

In an ideal situation, the server has tried most, if not all, of the bottles available by the glass, so they are your best resource. Ask them about what they like to drink and what they recommend. You'll surely learn a thing or two about sake (and the server!). At the very least, your server should be able to tell you which sakes are ordered the most—these will also be your freshest pours, as new bottles are opened more frequently. To get the peppiest drink possible, never hesitate to ask if a bottle has just been opened. This question is especially important with sparkling sakes or namas, where freshness is key. Ever get a flat glass of Champagne? Not cool!

Offer a Bit about Yourself

It is supremely helpful to tell the server about any preferences you might have; for example, that you "usually like something dry" or "have really been into fruity white wines lately"—these are great tidbits that can signal what you might like in the sake realm. Your server might suggest a minerally ginjo or honjozo for something dry, and for you "natty" lovers, a kimoto or yamahai.

Take Out Your Phone!

Photos speak volumes when you want a recommendation. We love it when a customer comes in and says, "I had this great sake the last time I was in Las Vegas," or "Do you have something like this?" and shows us a photo on their phone.

In the same vein, when you do take a picture of a bottle, it's best to capture both the front *and* back labels—whether they're in Japanese or English. This helps the shopkeeper or server because most of the information, including the name of the importer, is on the back label. And when you order a glass of sake at a restaurant, ask to see the bottle and take a picture of it! Labels are the gateways to decoding the bottles you like (see page 134 for more about labels).

Scrutinize the Menu

If the options on the menu are just "hot" or "cold" sake and you can't get any other information, there is probably less care and emphasis put on the sake menu at that establishment. A similar analogy would be a bar with just a "white" and "red" wine offered, with no information about the winery or name of the wine. Less care about selection can mean less attention to how the product is served.

However, if the establishment provides detailed information about all of their sakes (including the sake brewery and sake name or type), we urge you to explore all their options: cold, hot, and everything in between.

Are there multiple sakes or even a flight on the menu in addition to a few namas? Try some of them! These are the freshest brews available and usually go so well with food. Plus, this usually means that the sake buyer is paying attention to any new sakes that are available. If you're lucky and have a sake brewery in your town, there might even be a *namanama* sake, meaning completely unpasteurized.

Order by Temperature

Choose a cold ginjo or junmai daiginjo if you are craving a fruity aroma and soft, silky flavors in the glass. If you like a refreshing brewski after a long day, order a chilled honjozo or dry junmai, just as you would a crisp lager or pilsner! Try a full-bodied junmai or kimoto warmed up if you come into a cozy spot on a blustery day. Share a carafe of sake at room temperature with friends to make it merry! Since warm sake is best enjoyed when prepared with attention, we would choose a cold sake unless you are at an establishment where you know the sake will be served with care.

Pair the Sake with the Meal

Talk with your server about what you plan to order for your meal. You might want to start with a salad, go on to a pasta, and then a main dish. Do you want to order by the glass to try different sakes with various dishes, or would you rather get a bottle to take you all the way through dinner? Generally, we like to start with a nama or ginjo, then go on to a kimoto or junmai for the richer entrées. Finish with an aged sake for the dessert course.

Cork It!

If you're going somewhere that you know does not serve sake but you still want to try the restaurant's dishes with one, bring in a bottle and pay extra for the corkage.

Ordering for the Table?

Get a bottle! Bottles of sake are typically 720 ml (24 fluid ounces), about the same as a bottle of wine. You'll get about 6 pours per bottle, since sake pours are a tad smaller than wine. Another advantage of getting a bottle is that you know it's a fresh one, opened just for you.

PUT A SAKE IN YOUR CART

Selecting Sake at a Store

We're seeing more and more sakes at stores these days, which excites us to no end. Whether it's a grocery store or the corner wine shop, having sake as an option can really open up a whole new world for what to drink with dinner. But we also know that without proper guidance, sake shopping can be really confusing and even overwhelming, especially at something like a bigger box store, where none of the staff is trained in sake. We're here to help!

Drink Local

With more than twenty sake breweries throughout the U.S. (see Sake in the USA, page 135), there's a possibility you live near one. And if that's the case, your local shop might be carrying one of its bottles! Give it a shot—since a local brewery is closer than Japan, chances are the bottle is fresher.

Talk to a Salesperson Who Knows about Sake

Just like at a restaurant, there may be someone at the store who has enjoyed some of the bottles on the shelves. Don't be shy about asking for recommendations.

Eek! Don't Buy a Dusty Bottle

There's nothing sadder than an abandoned bottle of anything at the store, whether it's wine, mezcal, or your preferred olive oil. Because sake is brewed and has no preservatives, fresh is generally better. If you see dust, avoid it.

Try a One-Cup

One-cup sakes are 180 ml (6 fluid ounces) of sake packaged in aluminum cans or glass jars. Breweries market these as an on-the-go drink to pick up at train stations and *conbini* (convenience stores). They are perfect for picnics or ball games, or as mini accompaniments for snacks. They are also great for cooking when the recipe calls for just a little sake!

When in Doubt, Get the Ginjo!

Ginjos and junmai ginjos are the Goldilocks of sake (see Rule #4 on page 123). One of them will most often be just what you wanted—something a little fruity, light, food-friendly, and best served cold.

How to Read a Sake Label

Unfortunately, there is no standardized format for Japanese sake labels. One may have a lot of helpful info, including tasting notes and temperature suggestions, while another may have nothing more than the importer's name and ABV. Look for these hints to guide you toward a bottle you want to buy.

Sake Types + Rice Polish

If the label has the word *junmai* on it, that means the sake is made only with the classic ingredients: rice, water, koji, and yeast. If you don't see that word, then your sake is an aruten, meaning it has some added distilled alcohol.

When you see words like *ginjo* or *daiginjo,* you will know that the sake is using highly polished rice. Remember from chapter 1 that **the higher the rice-polishing ratio, the bolder and richer the sake. The lower the rice-polishing ratio, the more delicate and softer the texture.** And when you see a percentage on the bottle (other than the ABV), that is the percentage of rice that remains!

Refer to the chart on page 43 for more details about sake types, styles, and polish.

ABV (Alcohol by Volume)

Sakes are generally at 15 to 16% ABV, but some brewers will drop it down to 13 to 14%, especially during the summertime, to create lighter brews. Some sparkling or sweet sakes have a very low ABV (13% and under). Sakes higher than 17% will likely be weightier on the palate, bold, and rich. Many of these sakes are *genshus* (meaning undiluted) and express intense umami flavors, acidity, and complexity to balance the high alcohol content.

Sake in the USA

From Oregon to Arkansas, brewers across America are making sakes with their local communities in mind. The lack of specialized sake-making resources in the U.S. pushes brewers to adapt and innovate. This might mean using modified equipment made for beer brewing, or drawing on inspiration from local ingredients and beverages like horchata. Austin's Texas Sake Company infuses its junmai with oak chips to make a sake that pairs with good ol' Texas BBQ, while Arizona Sake in Holbrook brews a limited-edition sake made with prickly pear, the fruit that grows furiously throughout the desert.

While many brewers in the U.S. follow Japanese sake standards, there are no official standards here. Sake infused with oak chips or fruit would not be considered sake in Japan, but it can be in the States.

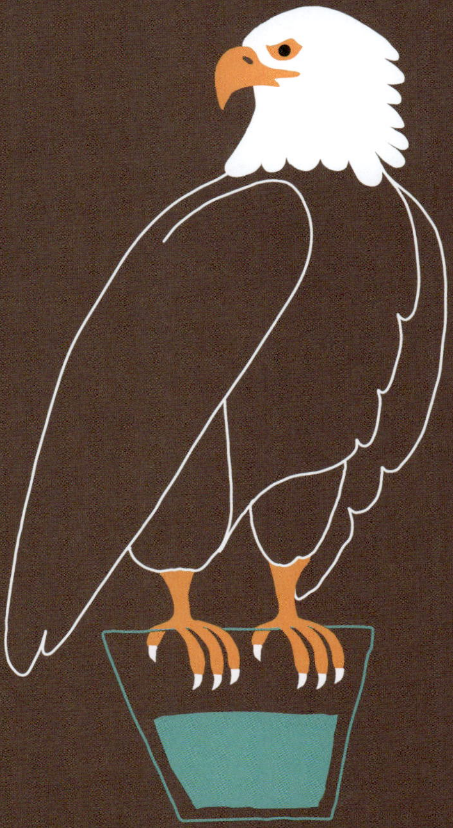

Cooking Sakes

We are often asked which sake would be ideal when the recipe you are making calls for a cup of sake. For cooking, we suggest getting the cheapest or smallest bottle or can of sake you can find. Remember that once opened, sake—even the kind you use for recipes—should always be stored in the fridge. While we try to finish sakes for drinking within one week of opening, we keep sakes for cooking in the fridge for up to two months.

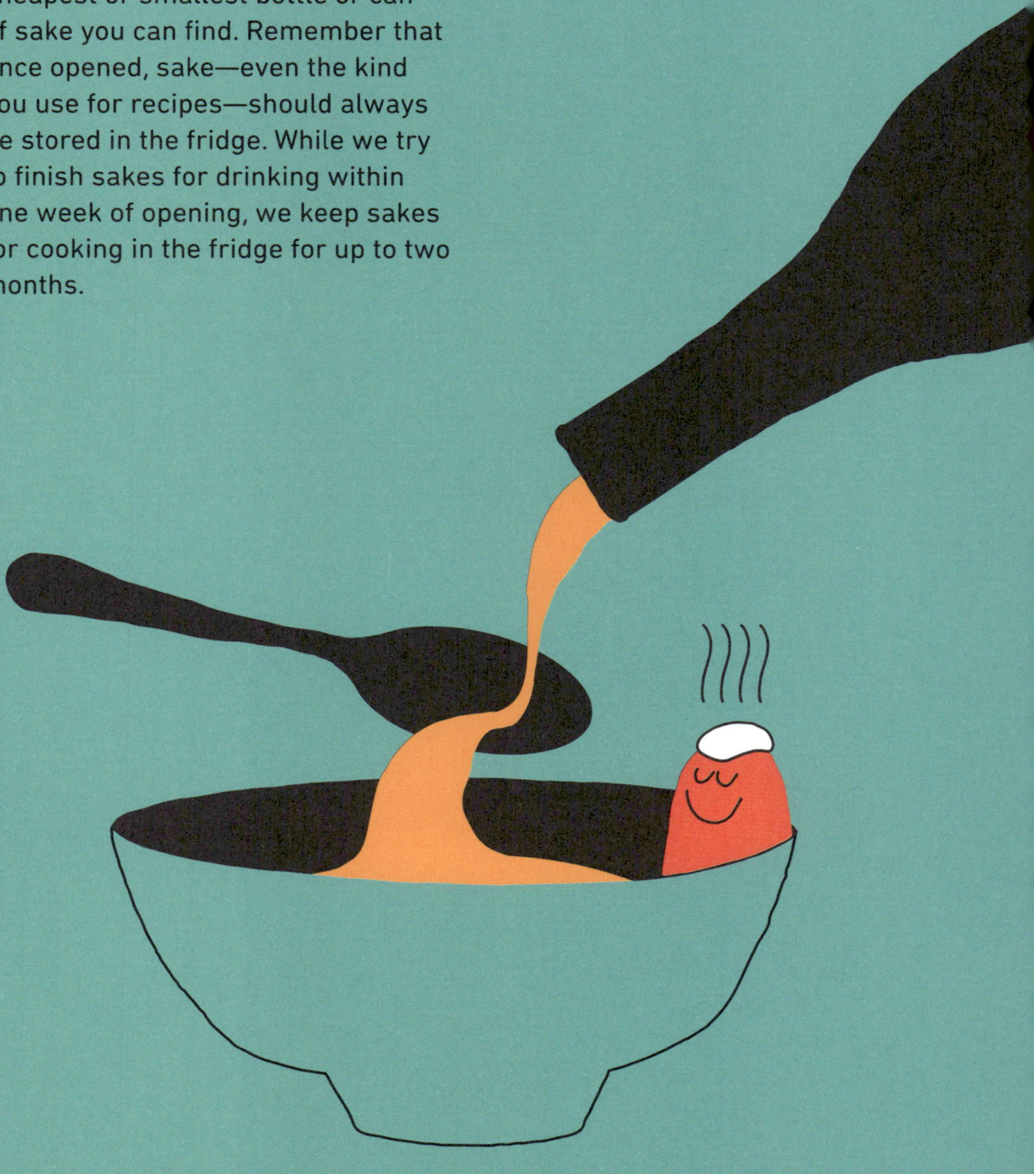

SMV (Sake Meter Value)

SMV, or Sake Meter Value, is a number you will often see on a bottle. It is a measure of the amount of sugar present in the sake, and it will give you an idea of whether the sake veers sweet or dry. The typical SMV range is −5 to +5. If the SMV is lower than −5 the sake will likely be sweet, while sakes with an SMV of +5 or higher will taste dry. However, there are many other factors that can skew how we perceive sweetness and dryness, such as acidity and aroma, so one must ultimately taste the sake to make the determination.

Acidity

You may see a number following the word "Acidity" on a label (acid can be found in all alcohols). The total acidity levels for sakes normally fall between 1.0 and 2.0, with the average around 1.3. For exactly what is being measured, we asked Yoshihiro Sako of Den Sake Brewery to explain: "It's the total acid for the sourness in sake (mainly lactic, succinic, malic, citric, and acetic acid) and also the level of CO_2, which heightens the effect of acidity on your palate."

Sake has about a fifth of the acidity of wine. Compared to sake, wines have much more of a "sour" effect, resulting in a drink that can function as a palate cleanser when having with richer, fattier dishes. With sake, because of its amino acids (see Amino Acid for more on that), the drink serves to enhance the flavors of your meal.

Read more about acidity in sake on page 98 of chapter 2, and see page 155 of chapter 4 for more on how it interacts with foods.

Amino Acid

You may also see a numerical value for amino acids on the label. Again, we turned to Sako for an explanation: "This measurement represents the amino acids released into the liquid when proteins from rice and koji are broken down by enzymes." Knowing the amino acid level may give you an idea of how savory or umami-forward a sake might taste. Most sakes have an amino acid value between 1.0 and 2.0. Anything lower than 1.0 is considered low in amino acids and may taste lighter—think Niigata's tanrei karakuchi (light and dry style). Sakes clocking in at 2.0 or higher are going to deliver a fuller, rich flavor.

Brewery or Importer

Recognize the name of the brewery or importer? There's a pretty good chance that if you liked their last bottle, you'll enjoy their other ones, too. We tell people to "follow the maker," especially when they are known to have a unique style and philosophy of sake brewing. We also know that sake importers often focus on a certain region or style, and when the company is headed by just one person, the sake portfolio is usually a reflection of their tastes.

Regions in Japan

If you're lucky, the bottle will have the name of the city or prefecture where the brewery is located. Knowing about a region's sake can give you an idea of how to pair it. We've highlighted some of the most famous sake-making regions, including their sake styles and well-known foods, in chapter 1 (see page 78).

Rice Type

Sometimes the name of the rice is listed on the label, which can give you some idea of what the sake will taste like. For example, Yamada Nishiki, considered "the King of Sake Rice," is often used to brew aromatic types like junmai daiginjos and daiginjos. Omachi, an heirloom sake rice, can create sakes that are grassy and herbaceous. See page 21 for a list of common sake rice varieties and their characteristics.

Date

More often than not, you'll see a year and month listed on the bottle, which is most likely the brew date. Remember that sake is best consumed fresh, so you're good if you're within two years of the printed date. The store is doing a great job if it's within the same year!

In Search of Organic

When customers ask for an organic sake, we ask them if they're looking for certified organic sake or sake made with organic ingredients. Finding certified organic sake is challenging, as getting certified can be costly. That's because in addition to using organic ingredients, the facility itself must be certified organic. JAS (Japanese Agricultural Standards) and USDA organic certifications are considered equivalent as of 2025, so look for these seals when you are on the hunt for organic sake.

If you are looking for sake made with organic or pesticide-free rice, however, there are many more options. Breweries that champion organic or pesticide-free sake rice include Moriki Shuzo, Tomita Shuzo, Tentaka Shuzo, and Chiyo Shuzo. Many of them take it a step further and use estate-grown rice so they know exactly how the rice has been grown.

We've visited Matsuse Shuzo numerous times and are impressed by their passion for the rice they use. Keizo Ishida, who heads the brewing team, has a hand in the whole rice sourcing process, including checking the condition of the rice that is cultivated with no chemical agents or fertilizers less than a five-minute drive from the brewery (read more on page 68 about minimal intervention sakes).

So the short answer is yes, organic sakes exist. But consider widening your search from certified organic sake to sake made with organic or pesticide-free rice.

A SAKE FOR EVERY DRINK LOVER

The world of sake is deep and vast and we think there is *just* the perfect sake for every drink enthusiast out there.

Toasting with Champagne? Try a Sparkling Sake!

Yes, they make sparkling sake, and the method of production is much like that of a pét-nat (naturally-carbonated) or canned sparkling wine (force-carbonated). We love to toast with a chilled sparkling sake in a flute. It pairs wonderfully with some fries and oysters. Kanpai!

We love: Kiuchi Awashizuku Sparkling, Nanbu Bijin AWA Sparkling, Uka Sparkling Organic Junmai Daiginjo

Can't Quit Crisp White Wines? Give Ginjos + Junmai Ginjos a Roll!

Like an easy, breezy Sauvignon Blanc, ginjo exhibits floral aromas with a crisp mouthfeel. Remember, ginjos tend not to be in one extreme or the other, making it an ideal sake to reach for when you want something that won't be polarizing.

We love: Bijofu Junrei Tama Junmai Ginjo, Suigei Koiku 54 Junmai Ginjo, Tenjin Bayashi Junmai Ginjo

Love an Aromatic Chardonnay? Go Steady with Daiginjos + Junmai Daiginjos!

While daiginjos and junmai daiginjos lack the oaky, buttery qualities of many Chardonnays, they are lush and full-bodied with big floral aromas, making them a great alternative. A daiginjo will wow in a big-bowled wine glass with its fruity aromas, and even more so if you can find a daiginjo nama.

We love: Aizu Homare Yamadanishiki Black Label Junmai Daiginjo Sake, Kuheiji Eau du Désir Junmai Daiginjo, Tedorigawa Kinka Gold Blossom Nama Arabashiri Daiginjo Sake

Fan of Full-Flavored Reds? Sip on Yamahai + Kimoto!

Made with traditional low-intervention styles of sake-brewing, yamahai and kimoto sakes are high in acidity due to the lactic acid that is produced naturally. We recommend these sakes for people who like to savor the earthy, yogurty, and sour flavors sometimes found in skin-contact wines and farmhouse ales.

We love: Amabuki Yamahai Junmai Omachi, Daishichi Rakutenmei Kioke Tokubetsu Junmai, Sohomare Tokubetsu Kimoto Junmai

Karakuchi + Onikoroshi

Usually the response we get from customers about what kind of sake they like is, "something dry." They might be recalling a sake they had once that was "too sweet," and most patrons assume they like dry sakes when they first walk through our doors.

Karakuchi, or dry, sakes emerged around the 1970s and '80s in Japan, along with the rise in popularity of ginjo sake. After the war ended in Japan, sanzoshu, a style of sake that had a boatload of additives in it in order to increase yield, became popular. Because of the scarcity of rice for sake-making, sanzoshu was a means to an end for a country desperate for booze. It was thick and sweet and—as we can only imagine—rough around the edges. Once the economy started booming again, however, people wanted higher-quality sakes, including any departure from the cloying sanzoshu.

There were two major developments in favor of karakuchi sakes: Asahi Super Dry beer and Niigata Tanrei, a style of sake formerly known as tanrei karakuchi. When Asahi's renowned beer debuted in 1987, people went nuts! And sake drinkers wanted their equivalent to this revolutionary concept of a "super dry" beverage.

Next there was the introduction of tanrei karakuchi sakes from Niigata, the sakes they are most known for throughout Japan. This region-specific style indicates sakes that are clean, crisp, and dry. Locals would also tell you that it's very food-friendly.

Remember those customers who told us they liked "something dry"? When we put together a flight with a dry sake next to a sweeter one, like a nama, more often than not the customer prefers the nama. Without the balance of sweetness, dry sakes can be perceived as rough and bitter (especially when tasted sans food). And don't sleep on the opportunity to try these sakes at a higher temperature—we think they are best when warmed.

Historically, onikoroshi sakes were considered to be so dry that even the toughest guy on the block would get drunk. But that didn't sound romantic enough, so instead it was eventually referred to as a sake that was so dry it would slay demons, or *onikoroshi*. With time, however, the discussion evolved beyond just the dryness or the increased SMV (Sake Meter Value) to encompass how a sake with heightened acidity pairs with heavier foods (typically served in the winter).

Committed to Natural Wines? Explore the World of Muroka Nama Genshus (MNG)!

For those who love a natty wine with high acidity, a muroka nama genshu (noncharcoal-filtered, unpasteurized, undiluted) will bring it all, at full intensity. These are best served cold or on ice!

We love: Akishika Omachi Yamahai Muroka Nama Genshu Junmai, Niida Honke Kinpou Shizenshu Kimoto Junmai, Terada Honke Musubi Muroka Nama Genshu Junmai

Grabbing a Pilsner? Quench Yourself with a Honjozo!

We call honjozo our "fridge door sake"—not too fruity, floral, or cloying, it's just easy to drink! We prefer it chilled in a wine glass.

We love: Atago no Matsu Honjozo, Kurosawa Junmai Kimoto, Matsunoi Tokubetsu Honjozo Sake

Belgian Beer Aficianado? Seek out a Bodaimoto or Mizumoto!

Those with a soft spot for ancient beer styles from European monastaries will appreciate a bodaimoto or mizumoto, two sakes made with a nearly obsolete method of production that results in sakes that are often funky, acidic, and full of umami. Bodaimoto was originally created at Shoryakuji Temple in Nara, where brewers still go to fetch the starter used to make this particular type of sake.

We love: Hanatomoe Mizumoto Muroka Genshu Junmai, Kamitaka Mizumoto Junmai Sake, Takacho Regal Hawk Bodaimoto Muroka Genshu Junmai

Crave Double IPAs? Ask for a Genshu!

Genshu is a tank-strength sake, meaning no water has been added for dilution—its concentrated, bold flavors will appeal to drinkers who crave strong, hoppy brews with a high ABV kick.

We love: Chochin 5055 Muroka Nama Genshu Junmai Ginjo, Murai Nigori Genshu, Narutotai Ginjo Nama Genshu Sake

Like Lagers? Grab a Junmai!

A junmai sake is easy to drink, just like a lager. Often with notes of steamed rice and custard, junmais are earthy, great at any temperature, and play nicely with all types of foods, from apps to main dishes, burgers to sushi.

We love: Brooklyn Kura Blue Door Junmai, Isojiman Pride of the Sea Shore Tokubetsu Junmai, Suigei Tokubetsu Junmai

Have a Sweet Tooth? Swirl a Nigori or Fruit Sake!

Nigoris are coarsely pressed sakes that can veer sweet and lower in ABV; they are often called "cloudy sake." "Coarsely pressed" means that some of the *sake kasu* (lees, the byproduct of pressing) are strained out during the pressing process, giving nigoris a cloudy, creamy texture, much like that of a Piña Colada. Fruit sakes are all the rage these days, clocking in at a lower ABV with flavors like yuzu, strawberry, and mango. These are perfect for sipping cold or with a splash of soda.

We love: Heiwa Tsuru-Ume Yuzu Sake, Maruishi Miwaku No Momo Sake, Yuki Otoko Snow Yeti Nigori Junmai Sake

Is Sherry Your Amour? Swipe Right on Koshus.

Koshus and kijoshus often exhibit oxidized notes of raisin and nuts or forest floor, just like sherry. Go ahead and enjoy them in a snifter at the end of the night.

We love: Hakkaisan Kijoshu, Ine Mankai Genshu Junmai, Mantensei Junmai Ginjo

Whisky Sipper? Retreat with a Taruzake!

Aged in cedar casks, taruzakes are dry with a faintly herbaceous, minty quality imparted from the wood. While taruzake does not taste anything like a whisky, we have found that whisky drinkers enjoy a glass of it, especially warmed up.

We love: Choryo Yoshinosugi no Taru Omachi Yamahai Junmai Sake, Hanatomoe Taru Maru Junmai, Kenbishi Mizuho Yamahai Junmai

Umeshu + Fruit Sake

While not technically considered sake because they violate the ingredient requirement, fruit-flavored sakes such as umeshu and yuzushu are a very popular offering. In addition to being low in alcohol, their sweeter, concentrated profiles can work well in a cocktail.

Umeshu has a flavor profile that people—from wine and sake drinkers to whisky connoisseurs—find pleasing and nostalgic. It's both sweet and tart with a distinct aroma of dried fruit. It's also one of the most satisfying summer drinks when served on the rocks or with a splash of soda.

Commercially produced umeshu has proved to be very popular in Japan. Consequently, umeshus with additives (artificial color and vitamin C) started to appear on the shelves. To differentiate these from additive-free umeshu, the category of *honkaku umeshu* (authentic umeshu) was established.

When Yoko lived in Tokyo, she had a glass of yuzu sake on a big block of ice every Friday night. In addition to yuzu sakes, all types of citrus-infused sakes were common in bars (daidai, mikan, sudachi, etc). Today, strawberry, yuzu, and peach are just some of the popular fruit sakes available—preserving fruit like this is a common way to enjoy fresh, abundant flavors all year long.

Wanna Keep It Low-ABV?
Sparkling, Natsuzake, or Sake Highball, Please!

Sparkling sakes are good choices for people looking for a low-ABV refreshment, as they tend to have more residual sugars and ABVs that hover around 10%, some even going as low as 5%. A newer seasonal style called *natsuzake* (summer sake) refers to sakes that are light, crushable, and best enjoyed ice-cold. These sakes, which are often unpasteurized, have an ABV of around 10 to 13%. While it may seem counterintuitive to grab a genshu as a low-ABV option, we do so when we want to make a low-ABV sake highball. A genshu that has an ABV of 17 to 20% will retain its flavor in a highball, but the drink ends up being lower in alcohol because the sake is diluted by plenty of ice and soda.

We love: Daisekkei Summer Light Junmai Nama Genshu, Koueigiku Tasogare Twilight Orange Muroka Nama Genshu Highball, Sawa Sawa Nigori Sparkling Sake

Ordering a Martini?
A Karakuchi or Onikoroshi Will Do Just as Well!

If you are craving a refreshingly dry drink, look for the words *karakuchi* or *onikoroshi* on the label. The *kara* in karakuchi means "dry" or "spicy," while *kuchi* means "mouth" or "taste." *Onikoroshi* means "demon slayer," as these sakes are said to be so dry they will kill demons. All of these sakes are usually grain-forward and savory rather than fruity and floral, with a telltale spicy ending. A dry, spicy finish works particularly well with fried foods and salty tapas-style dishes. If you want to mellow out the spice, warm the sake up a little.

We love: Imayo Tsukasa Black Extra Dry Junmai, Kikusui Karakuchi Honjozo, Shishi no Sato Chokara Onikoroshi Junmai Sake

SAKE MOOD RING

Whatever your mood, there's a sake for it!

ROMANTIC • BUBBLY

*Wine and dine me with something **sparkling**!*

FANCY • FLORAL

*Just got a raise, impress me with a **daiginjo**!*

SMITTEN • SWEET

*Pour me some **nigori** and gaze into my eyes.*

WANNA PARTY? • FRUITY

*Feeling as fresh as a **nama**. How do I look?*

ADVENTUROUS • BOLD

*Explore uncharted territories with a **tokubetsu junmai**.*

TIRED • CRISP

*Put a pep in my step with a **honjozo**.*

STRESSED • STIFF

*Shut up and get me a glass of **genshu**.*

CONTEMPLATIVE • AGED

*Lemme think about it over a glass of **kijoshu**.*

COZY • EARTHY

*Staying in and puzzling all night with some **junmai** in my favorite mug.*

MYSTERIOUS • UMAMI

*Craving something mystical and steeped in tradition—I'll try a **kimoto,** warmed up.*

PAIR

SAKE + FOOD

Sake is full of umami. It is this very fact that makes sake an ideal beverage for food pairing, because umami is known to enhance other flavors. Combining different umami-rich foods creates a flavor explosion—for example, when we mix kombu and bonito flakes in water, we get a rich-flavored dashi that seems to have exponential umami. But the perception of sweet and salty flavors also seems to be enhanced by umami. So when we sip on an umami-rich sake, it can pull out the sweetness in other ingredients and the saltiness in sauces, making food taste even more vivid and flavorful.

During the Edo period, a small mound of salt was sometimes dusted onto a corner of a *masu* (square wooden box), to be licked while sipping on the sake. Izumi Motai, formerly of Takara Sake USA (Berkeley), explained to us that this practice was likely addressing the fact that saltiness is the only missing flavor in sake, and that salt enhances the sweetness and umami of sake. This was most certainly the start of more complex sake pairings, like a smear of miso or salty pickles.

Similar pairings are still served in Tokyo today. We visited Toshimaya Shuzo, one of the oldest sake shops in Tokyo, which has been operating since 1596. The president of Toshimaya Shuzo, Toshiyuki Yoshimura, told us the custom all started when customers wanted to taste their sake, so they opened a bar and restaurant offering little bites. Their most popular item was tofu spread with miso, and it is still on the menu at their sake shop in Kanda, Tokyo.

As Japanese cuisine has developed, so has sake. From legacy brewers like Kenbishi and Otokoyama to newer sake-makers like Tenbi and Dassai, all are in agreement: Sake is made to support food. Think of sake as the best supporting actor, with the food as the best actor. While the actors in supporting roles can shine and win awards, they are aware that they would not exist without the lead.

Wine and food pairings work by cleansing and resetting the palate with wine after tasting bites of food. This satisfying seesaw effect is possible mainly because of the acid present in wine. After eating something rich, buttery, or cheesy, a sip of wine gives you a burst of tart acidity that can rinse away those rich flavors.

Sake and food pairings work differently from wine pairings. The umami in sake enhances the flavors of food. Therefore, rather than a seesaw effect, there's a synergy in the mouth that takes place when sipping on sake and savoring food—especially foods with umami. The low acidity of sake also plays well with many foods, especially seafood, and prevents clashes in food pairings.

Traditional Japanese foods including sashimi, soba, and grilled fish are generally light, high in umami, and low in spice and fat. But Japanese cuisine doesn't include just these lighter dishes. Many dishes adopted from other cuisines since the 1500s, when the Portuguese first arrived in Nagasaki, are richer or include spices that are not native to Japan: think tempura from Portugal, hambagu from Germany, curry from India by way of the British, ramen from China, and croquettes from France. Many of these dishes have been around for so long that they are now considered Japanese. Thus, sake has developed alongside a breadth of flavors and can pair with a range of foods, from lighter ones like sushi to the bold flavors of ramen and hambagu.

Fast-forward to present-day Tokyo and you'll find that restaurants and grocery stores are up on all the new food trends and flavors from around the world, promoting offerings that are richer than the traditional Japanese diet. Tapas bars featuring the best pintxos and Michelin-starred New Nordic restaurants are more common in Tokyo (population 14 million) than New York City (population 8 million)—and many have sake on their beverage lists. Chefs and sake-makers are evolving their menus and their sakes with each other in mind, which leaves the mandate of "sake with sushi" in the rearview mirror. To complement these newer flavors, sake-makers are experimenting with different kojis, higher fermentation temperatures, and newer yeasts.

This is an exciting time for sake, when a customer can walk into our store and whether they are having paella or a burger for dinner, we'll have a recommendation at the ready.

HOW SAKE INTERACTS WITH FLAVORS

Savory + Umami

Sake and umami go hand in hand. Pairing sake with foods that are also high in amino acid enhances the umami of both—often leading to the discovery of a third flavor that could be unlocked only when having them together.

One of our favorite food pairings with sake is cheese, which is high in umami. Every year, we have an event called Sakqueso, where we pair cheeses with different sakes. It is always a great experiment, as unexpected third flavors often emerge from the pairings. Standout pairings have included a dry kimoto sake with Mimolette, which resulted in a malty flavor that reminded us of the most delicious Dorito chip! We've also enjoyed a decadent pairing of a red rice sake with a spruce-wrapped, bloomy-rind cow's milk cheese that somehow tasted just like a New York–style raspberry cheesecake.

Foods that are high in umami and low in fat, such as asparagus and mushrooms, are great candidates for pairing with honjozos, junmai ginjos, and daiginjos. These sakes have low acidity and mild bitterness and can pull out flavors from foods that have inherent umami but not a lot of fat content. This is one of sake's superpowers—it can make lighter foods taste exceptionally delicious because of the heightened perception of umami.

Red meat is known for its high umami content, making it a great contender for a sake pairing. Do not miss the opportunity to pair juicy rib eye steak or slices of grilled Wagyu with a sake. With a higher fat content than seafood, these meats pair best with sakes that have higher levels of acidity and plenty of amino acids, like yamahai junmais and kimotos. These sturdy sakes have enough acidity to stand up against the rich meats, but they also provide lots of umami to highlight the umami in the meat. Our mouths are watering already!

Fried + Savory

Cold sparkling sakes and dry honjozos are ideal accompaniments to fries, tempura, karaage, and corn fritters. The bubbles and refreshing finish of the sake will cleanse your palate for the next crispy bite.

Balance a grazing board of salty snacks like cured meats, smoked oysters, and olives with a room-temperature genshu or full-bodied kimoto. The bold, acidic notes of the sake will stand up to such rich, savory flavors, and the umami of the sake will enhance the savory elements of these foods.

Acidic

Fresh tomatoes and salads dressed with vinegar can be accentuated by the fruity flavors of a nama or ginjo with high levels of malic acid. These bright, fruitier sakes can bring out the sweetness in tangy produce like fresh tomatoes, beets, and corn, while mellowing out the acidity in vinaigrettes and fermented foods. Look out for namas, junmai ginjos, or ginjos made with experimental yeasts like No. 28 or flower yeasts that produce a lot of malic acid.

Pair pizza and pastas with tomato sauce with sakes that have high levels of acidity (2.0 or more) and high sweetness (look for an SMV, or Sake Meter Value, of less than 0) or sakes made with white koji. If the sake's acidity levels are too low (anything less than 1.5), it will feel flat and get lost. We've seen junmais and junmai ginjos that match high acidity with more sugar to mimic the flavors of wine. The juiciness of the sake stands up to the acidity of the sauce and creaminess of the cheese on a pizza. Another way we are seeing brewers dial up acidity is by using white koji, which produces citric acid. The lemony flavors from the citric acid in the sake echo the tartness of tomato sauces.

Hot + Spicy

Low-alcohol sakes and nigoris can be paired with foods that have lots of spicy heat: Dishes like kimchi, tan tan ramen (a spicy Sichuan-Japanese noodle dish), or pad krapow gai (spicy Thai basil chicken) can result in that sizzling-hot sensation in your mouth. Smother the burn with a mild, milky, sweet nigori.

You can also enhance that burning sensation that some people enjoy by pairing your spicy food with a crisp, cold, dry honjozo or junmai. These types of sake will accentuate the spice instead of tamping it down.

Spiced

Rustic bodaimotos or koshus with high acid and sweetness have proved to be a winning pairing with spiced dishes like awaze tibs (Ethiopian lamb stew) and barbecued meats. The tart, sweet, and earthy flavors in these sakes are similar to those of tej (Ethiopian honey wine) and bring out the dynamic flavors of berbere, cumin, coriander, and other spices.

Dishes made with earthy, tongue-numbing Szechuan peppercorns are a zesty pairing with rustic sakes like *kioke jikomi* (sake fermented in traditional cedar tubs) and *taruzake* (sake aged in cedar barrels). The woody aroma of these sakes draws out the floral characteristic of this distinctive pepper.

The Origins of Umami

The word *umami* is derived from the Japanese characters 旨い (*umai*, meaning delicious) and 味 (*mi*, meaning taste). It was discovered in 1908 by Dr. Kikunae Ikeda, who wanted to pinpoint the flavors present in his daily bowl of miso soup. He was able to isolate the glutamic acid from the kombu that is used to make the dashi for the soup. Umami was officially recognized as one of the five basic taste senses by the international scientific community in 1985; it is best defined as meaty, brothy, and mouthwatering.

Sweet

Koshus (aged sakes) and kijoshus are ideal with desserts. Similar to port or sherry, koshus are darker in color, viscous, sweet, and best enjoyed at room temperature at the end of a meal. A koshu will bring out the complex bitterness of dark chocolate or the earthiness of a plate of cheeses.

We've found that saltiness is an important element in dessert pairings with sakes like koshu and kijoshu that are high in both sugars and umami. For example, if you want to pair sake with dark chocolate, opt for a salted chocolate. Without the salt, the nuances of the chocolate can fall flat against the sake. Use the same concept for a cheese plate; choose aged, salty cheeses to contrast with the sweet sake. Koshu and kijoshu also work well with salted caramel ice cream and confections. We recommend pairing a lighter dessert, like a bowl of berries or even a fresh peach, with a nama or sparkling sake that has aromas of bright fruit. These fruity sakes can enhance the acidity in fresh fruits and make them taste juicier.

Creamy desserts made with dairy are best paired with a mellow, easy-to-drink yamahai or kimoto, both of which have creaminess and rich umami characteristics from the lactic acid. While it's tempting to pair a cheesecake, chocolate mousse, or buttery shortbread cookie with a sweet sake, we've found that a no-frills junmai that is neither overly fruity nor overly sweet pairs best. The dairy in the dessert is enhanced by the lactic acid and umami of the sake and doesn't need anything else to get in its way.

FOOD PAIRINGS

We've been drinking sake with our meals for decades now and have learned that there is a sake for every dish or cuisine. Remember that sake is made to pair with food, and nowadays brewers are keeping global flavors in mind when creating their sakes. There are no hard-and-fast rules about which sakes to drink with specific dishes. Rather, you should drink what you like, how you like! That said, there *are* sakes we can suggest that pair especially well with certain foods.

With so many different styles and bottles out there, where do you start? From pairings for special-occasion omakase dinners to simple weeknight meals, we have you covered.

PAIRING BY INGREDIENT

Vegetables

Tomato / Eggplant

These summery nightshades pair well with a fruitier style of sake like a **nama** or **junmai ginjo** that bring out the sweetness of the vegetable.

Beans / Tofu

Enjoy hummus or fresh tofu with a **taruzake**—its dry, minty fragrance enhances the earthiness of legumes (e.g., chickpeas or soybeans).

Herbs

A crisp, subtle **honjozo** will help garnishes like parsley, marjoram, and thyme shine in your dishes.

Shiitake / Porcini

Pair savory mushrooms with an umami-forward sake like a **yamahai** or **kimoto,** and you will be rewarded with an umami explosion.

Broccoli Rabe / Kale

Mellow out the bitter flavors of dark greens with a **junmai daiginjo** or **daiginjo,** both of which tend to be low in acidity and big in fruit flavor.

Potato / Carrot

Dial up the earthiness of root vegetables with mineral-forward **murokas,** which often have earthy aromas as well.

Cheese

Mozzarella / Gouda

Try a fruity **ginjo** with a classic, mellow cow's milk cheese—an easy pairing that's a welcome sight after you come home from work. As a sashimi alternative, try dipping mozzarella into soy sauce and wasabi with a glass.

Chèvre / Feta

We love a tangy cheese with an acidic **yamahai** or **kimoto**. The elements of tartness play nicely with one another.

Camembert / Brie

You can't lose by pairing a rich, creamy cheese with a floral **daiginjo**. The sake's bouquet can highlight the nuanced flavors in cheeses like Camembert and Brie. It'll convince anyone to consider a sake at their next "wine and cheese" party.

Gruyère / Cheddar

The nuttiness of aged cheese is highlighted by **aged sakes,** creating the ultimate umami bomb.

PAIRING BY INGREDIENT

Seafood

Halibut / Snapper

For a lighter fish, choose a crisp **ginjo** or **junmai ginjo** that won't get in the way of a delicate flavor and texture.

Tuna / Salmon

Choose a rich **junmai** to pair with meatier fish: with raw fish, serve the sake chilled, so the cold fish isn't a shock to the palate. With a cooked fillet, a sake at room temperature or warmed will enhance the umami of the fish.

Clams / Oysters / Crab / Shrimp

Match briny, umami-laden shellfish with the elegance of a **daiginjo** or a crisp **honjozo.** The salinity of raw oysters is ideal against a daiginjo's subtle aromas, while cooked or grilled bivalves are delicious with a lighter honjozo. You can't go wrong with this winning combination of umami-on-umami!

Anchovy / Sardines / Mackerel

Pack a punch with a bold **genshu** or tart **bodaimoto** to match the intensity of oily fish with strong aromas.

Meat

Chicken

A rice-forward **junmai ginjo** will dial up the lighter, more delicate flavors of chicken.

Pork

We love a lively **nama** to enhance the richness and sweetness of pork in dishes like tonkotsu ramen, *nabe* (hot pot), and simmered pork belly.

Beef

Enjoy an acid-forward, robust **yamahai** or **kimoto** to accent heartier, savory beef dishes and refresh your palate.

Lamb / Duck

We love a hazy, slightly sweet **nigori** against the funkier flavors of game meats.

PAIRING BY DISHES

Fresh Seafood

Ceviche, grilled salmon, shrimp cocktail

Go with a **ginjo** alongside sushi or oysters on the half shell. The refreshing fruitiness of a ginjo or **junmai ginjo** will bring out the delicate flavors of fish and the brininess of crustaceans.

All-American

Mac + cheese, chili, pizza delivery

Try a **junmai**! These sakes are sturdy and versatile. The rice-forward flavors deliver lots of umami, which will complement an equally umami-heavy pepperoni pizza, or a plate of spaghetti and meatballs.

Off the Grill

BBQ, yakitori, burgers

If you are firing up the grill, grab a dry **junmai** and serve it chilled. Look for the words ***karakuchi, otokoyama,*** or ***onikoroshi*** on the label, which denote a dry style. They will be what you crave while you get your hands sticky with sweet and salty *tare* (grilling sauce made with soy sauce, mirin, and sugar) or a rich BBQ sauce.

Fried fare: tempura, fried chicken, po' boys

Craving something battered and fried? Try a bottle of **honjozo**. With subdued aromas, these refreshingly crisp sakes cut the grease between bites of fried fish, shellfish, or vegetables.

Funky meats: duck confit, lamb curry, charcuterie, tacos

Gamey meats pair wonderfully with a **bodaimoto, yamahai,** or **kimoto**. The acidity and tart flavor of these sakes will balance out any funk (the good kind!) in your food.

PAIRING BY DISHES

Spicy

Korean fried chicken, jerk shrimp, pad thai

Nigoris work best with spicy foods, as their rich texture and sweetness can tamp down the heat. Choose a milky nigori as a pairing for hearty spiced stews or dishes drizzled with hot sauce.

Spices of the World

Paella, chicken tikka masala, dan dan mein

While **namas** are not necessarily "one-size-fits-all," their punchy, fresh flavors go well with richly spiced dishes and Mediterranean flavors.

Dessert

Chocolate, cake

A deep-colored ***koshu*** (aged sake) would be a nice candidate to sip alongside salted chocolate chip cookies or carrot cake. The caramel-like flavors of the sake are all the more satisfying with salty, savory flavors. For fruit desserts like pies, an ***usunigori*** (light nigori) will enhance the sweetness of the fruit without overpowering it.

Sake + Fish

We have noticed that salmon tastes fresh with sake but fishy with red wine. We always knew that sake has the edge over wine when it comes to seafood pairings, but why?

To answer this question, we enlisted the help of food science writer Harold McGee. Harold told us that the tinny, metallic flavor you taste when drinking wine with salmon comes from the iron in the wine, which breaks up the polyunsaturated fats in the fish. It turns out that the processing equipment used in winemaking is full of iron, as is the soil that the grapes grow in. Inevitably, iron ends up in the wine. While red wine has a higher iron content than white, the latter still contains some iron—so the lack of iron in sake makes it optimal for pairing with seafood. In fact, as we mentioned in chapter 1, brewers specifically choose water low in iron for sake-making.

PAIRING BY SAKE

Sparkling

Raw oysters, fries

Try a **sparkling sake** instead of Champagne to kick off a meal or celebrate a special occasion with some small bites. Or feel free to pop one open on any night—we do love sparkling sake with greasy foods (especially if it's a sparkling nigori!).

Daiginjo + Junmai Daiginjo

Sashimi, tofu poke bowl

Quintessential **daiginjo** aromas include melon and green apple, which tend to pair well with lighter dishes that won't overwhelm the subtle qualities of the sake.

Ginjo + Junmai Ginjo

Caesar salad, roasted chicken

Chilled **ginjos** are often enjoyed with lighter foods such as vegetables or poultry, as the refreshing fruitiness of these sakes brings out the delicate flavors of those foods. That said, there are plenty of ginjos available that lean savory and can be paired with bolder dishes, too.

Honjozo

Onion rings, deviled eggs

Honjozos are our go-to sake for casual feasts. Their refreshingly crisp style, with subdued aromas, cuts the oil and resets the palate between bites of fried fish, pickles, and salami. Best enjoyed with some nibbles—either chilled, or better yet, at room temperature or warmed up—honjozos are easy to drink and a flexible pairing for many dishes.

Junmai

Steak, potstickers

Sturdy and versatile, **junmais** can stand up to bold dishes and ingredients. Their rich grain flavors deliver lots of umami, which will complement equally umami-heavy meals! Warm up a junmai to enhance its full-bodied, rice-forward flavors and experience a cozy pairing with steaming-hot rich dishes.

PAIRINGS BY SAKE

Yamahai + Kimoto

Peking duck, mushroom pizza

An acidic, tart **yamahai** or **kimoto** is an excellent accompaniment to a grand meal. The tart, yogurty notes will balance richness or gamier flavors.

Nama

Hot dogs, veggie chow mein

Many **genshus** and **namas** are bold, assertive, and layered, which opens up a bunch of possibilities for pairing them with street foods that you may have at a ball game or night market. These bottles are oftentimes effervescent, which adds a contrasting, dynamic texture and tingle to the pairing.

Taruzake

Hummus, cornbread

Since **taruzake** has minty notes from being aged in cedar casks, it pairs well with simple foods, snacks, or dishes made with fresh herbs. We love munchin' on nuts with a cup of taruzake.

Nigori

Buffalo wings, tacos

These days, there's a **nigori** for everyone, with options ranging from sweet and syrupy to relatively dry and incredibly savory. Depending on your tolerance level for sweets, the right nigori can be a home-run pairing with spicy and grilled foods. We like to serve a moderately sweet nigori alongside spicy foods and have a dry one as another option for saucy dishes.

Koshu

Braised pork, tiramisu

Aged sakes are known for deep flavors ranging from mushrooms and soy sauce to plums and spiced apples. While they are commonly served with desserts, we find that rich, savory dishes also make wonderful pairings.

EVERYDAY SAKE

A SAKE FOR EVERY DAY OF THE WEEK

DAY	SAKE
Monday	nama or junmai ginjo
Tuesday	junmai or kimoto
Wednesday	nigori
Thursday	junmai
Friday	honjozo
Saturday	sparkling, daiginjo
Sunday	sake highball, amazake

PAIRING

We often start our weeknight meals, especially on Meatless Monday, with something light and easy to prep, like braised beans and a leafy green salad with avocado and a vinaigrette.

Grilled fish with pickles or roasted chicken on a bed of vegetables are always on rotation.

Life gets busy, so hump day may mean Chinese takeout or taco night!

Noodles are our carb of choice, whether it's pasta Bolognese or a bowl of steaming ramen.

After a long week, simply snacking on some cheese, finger foods, and olives is in order.

We like to celebrate the weekend with a temaki party in the summer or hot pot with friends in the winter. Either way, the meal is leisurely, and we take the time to pair one of our sakes with each course.

Boo-hoo, the weekend is over! We like a low-alcohol or nonalcoholic option to reset for the new week ahead.

SAKE FOR ANY OCCASION

Sake is always an excellent party starter, and we love bringing it to all kinds of outings and events. People are often intrigued, so there is no shortage of conversation and never any awkward silences. As a new expert on sake, you should be prepared to answer inquiries like, "What is a nama?," "Is sake rice wine?," and "Is hot sake bad?" (See page 191 for the answer!)

Picnics + BBQ

There's nothing like cold **ginjos** or **namas** to pair with grilled meats and veg, pasta salads, and snacks al fresco. If it's the middle of summer, try seeking out *natsuzake* (a seasonal summer sake), which is a touch lower in alcohol and best served ice-cold (think of it as a refreshing lagers).

We love: Hakurakusei Junmai Ginjo, Ryusei Ryofu Junmai Ginjo Nama

Dinner Party

Nothing brings the party like a bottle of Muroka Nama Genshu, or **MNG**. Noncharcoal-filtered (or *muroka*), unpasteurized (or *nama*), and tank-strength (or *genshu*), this sake is bold, fruity, and vivacious—strap yourself into your nicest shoes and bring your A-game to stand up to this one. Remember to have the bottle prechilled for immediate enjoyment.

We love: Kaze no Mori Wind of the Woods Muroka Nama Genshu Junmai, Noguchi Muroka Nama Genshu Honjozo Sake

Holiday Feast

Bring something different to Thanksgiving or Christmas this year! We've found that **yamahais + kimotos** have the acidity to balance rich dishes like ham or turkey with gravy. Or take advantage of the *hiyaoroshi* (seasonal fall sakes) that exhibit flavors like persimmon, mushroom, warm spice, and oak, and start hitting the shelves in October.

We love: Mana 1751 True Vision Yamahai Tokubetsu Muroka Genshu Junmai Sake, Shichi Hon Yari Junmai Hiyaoroshi

Wedding

Considered to be in the highest echelon of celebration drinks, sake is always consumed at weddings in Japan. To start, we recommend a floral, opulent **daiginjo** (perhaps with gold flakes?), then a fruity ginjo to take you into the dance party.

We love: Kanbara Bride of the Fox Junmai Ginjo, Kamotsuru Tokusei Gold Daiginjo

Book Club

Need something that will keep the conversation going, perhaps even start a debate or two? We like a refreshing **honjozo** or dry **junmai** for discussions about serious (or lowbrow) literature.

We love: Yuki Otoko Snow Yeti Honjozo, Everlasting Roots Tokubetsu Junmai

Anniversary Dinner

Kanpai to another year (or decade!) with a fragrant sake like **daiginjo** or a **sparkling sake** in a flute!

We love: Chiyomusubi Daiginjo, Hakkaisan Yukimuro 3 Year Junmai Daiginjo

Sports Games

Honjozos pair super well with halftime favorites like chicken wings and nachos. We have a customer who loves to drink **namas** with a bucket of fried chicken! If you're actually going to a game, one-cups are perfect for no-nonsense enjoyment while cheering on your favorite baseball, football, or soccer team.

We love: Eiko Fuji 10,000 Ways Honjozo, Asabiraki Namacho Honjozo

Brunch

Add some **sparkling sake** to orange juice or a bold **genshu** to your Bloody Mary served alongside Eggs Benedict or French toast!

We love: Shirakabegura Mio Sparkling, Suehiro Poochi Poochi Sparkling Sake

Sushi Party

We give a lot of sake advice to people going to sushi dinners, and we usually suggest a **daiginjo** or **junmai ginjo,** both of which tend to pair well with the subtle, light flavors of Japanese cuisine.

We love: Otokoyama Sushi Booster Junmai, Saika Yamada Nishiki Junmai Daiginjo

High School Reunion

Catch up with your besties over a glass of **nama** or a lively **ginjo**—the fruity boldness will get the night going and the party won't stop until you say so!

We love: Tenbu Junmai Ginjo, Brooklyn Kura Nama Chozo Junmai Ginjo Occidental Dry Hopped Sake

After-Party

For a nightcap, there's nothing like a pensive aged sake like **koshu** to round out the evening. With flavors that range from sherry to mushrooms, these sakes are the perfect segue to the next stop: your beloved bed.

We love: Kisoji Sanwari Koji Junmai, Prince Nagaya Junmai

HOST A SAKE COCKTAIL PARTY

Sakes have a range of flavors that you can incorporate into cocktails, from citrus or stone fruit to mushroomy umami or whether stirred or shaken.

Opt for fr
strawberr

Substitute sake for the v
in three-ingredient cock
martinis and Manha

For creamier textures and rice-
forward flavors, use a nigori.

Use a nama for freshness with apple or melon flavors—plus, it may be a bit effervescent!

ike yuzu or
flavor profiles.
Substitute sparkling sake for
sparkling wine or Champagne.
Try genshu sakes, as
their bolder flavors
will come through
better thanks to the
higher ABV.
Make it a low-ABV cocktail
by flipping the ratios—
i.e., more sake to spirits.
Since sake is quite subtle,
stir or shake your cocktail
for less time so the flavors
do not get diluted.
Or keep it simple
and enjoy sake
on the rocks!

GO-TO SIMPLE COCKTAIL RECIPES

Saketini

Lovers of dry martinis should try this updated cocktail with a hint of umami.

1.5 ounces of your favorite gin
1.5 ounces honjozo sake
Lemon twist, for serving

Stir the gin and sake together in a mixing glass with plenty of ice for 20 to 30 seconds. Strain into a coupe. Garnish with the lemon twist.

Sake Highball

Quench your thirst with this refreshing soda served in a Collins glass after a long week.

3 ounces nama genshu sake
5 ounces club soda

Pour the sake into a tall glass with ice, followed by the club soda. Gently stir to incorporate.

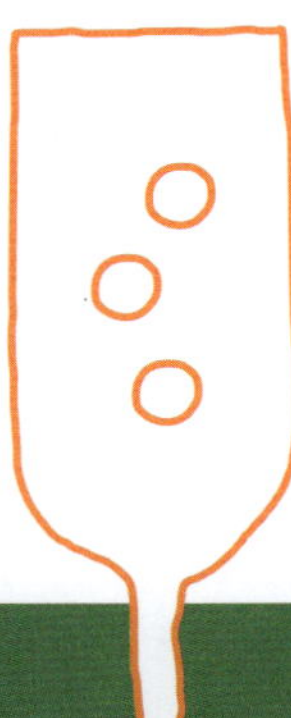

Tokyo 75

Enjoy this fresh take on a brunch classic, the French 75.

1 ounce gin
0.5 ounce fresh lemon juice
Barspoon of simple syrup
2 ounces sparkling sake
Lemon twist, for garnish

Pour the gin, lemon juice, and simple syrup into a cocktail shaker and shake for 10 seconds. Strain into a coupe and top with the sparking sake. Garnish with the lemon twist.

Samurai Lime

3 ounces nama genshu sake
0.5 ounce fresh lime juice
0.25 ounce simple syrup
Lime wedge

In a cobbler shaker, combine the sake, lime juice, and simple syrup. Add ice and shake for 15 seconds. Strain into a rocks glass and garnish with the lime wedge.

SERVE

氷
酒
甘

TEMPERATURE

One thing unique to sake is the wide range of temperatures at which you can enjoy it. But it can sometimes be confusing. When should you serve sake cold and when should you warm it up? Is sake ever heated to mask low quality?

When we get asked these questions, we like to draw parallels with other drinks like beer and wine. Crisp, light styles like lagers, Sauvignon Blancs, and sparkling wines are served chilled to emphasize the refreshing and fruity characteristics of these drinks, while fuller-bodied, complex styles like stouts, Cabernet Sauvignons, and ports are ideal at higher temperatures so you can taste the spectrum of flavors the drink has to offer.

The same goes for sake—fruity, crisp namas, ginjos, and daiginjos are best served chilled to enhance their fresh aromas, while the fuller-bodied umami flavors in junmais, kimotos, and aged sakes are better detected when they are served at room temperature or warmed.

In general, light styles tend to be served colder, while fuller styles are best enjoyed at a higher temperature. To illustrate this temperature range, refer to the chart opposite.

Sake	Temp	Why	How
Sparkling	Very cold: 40°F	To preserve effervescence and emphasize refreshing texture.	Keep in the coldest part of the fridge; pour into chilled glasses and serve immediately
Low-alcohol, nama	Cold: 45°F	To preserve fresh fruitiness. If the temperature gets too high, low-alcohol sakes may lose their crispness and taste too sweet.	Keep in the main part of the fridge; pour and serve immediately.
Daiginjo, ginjo	Chilled: 50° to 55°F	Similar to the reasons given above—cooler temperatures preserve crisp acidity and fruity aromatics. If these sakes are served too warm, they can taste flat.	Keep in the main part of the fridge; remove 10 minutes before serving.
Honjozo, junmai, kimoto, yamahai, aged	Room temp: 60° to 70°F	Serving these sakes at close to room temperature reduces any bitterness and acidity associated with the higher alcohol content. Higher temperatures allow complex, savory aromas to be more detectable.	If these are stored unopened in a cool, dark place, serve at your leisure. If stored in the refrigerator, bring to room temperature 30 minutes before serving.
Honjozo, junmai, kimoto, yamahai, aged	Warmed: 105° to 120°F	Serving these styles warmed can emphasize the umami, nuttiness, and spice, while mellowing out any sharpness in the finish.	Warm in a carafe or mugs in a hot water bath. See page 192 for how to warm sake.

Sake Forecast

Whether you're under the blazing sun with sticky humidity or in a raging snowstorm, there's a sake to enjoy at any temperature! Sake is versatile in the way it is served, so you can have an icy-cold nama ginjo when it's hot outside and sip on a warm kimoto junmai when it's cold.

Sake for Warm Weather

It's time to bring out some ice-cold, refreshing sake to beat the heat! We love smaller-format sakes like one-cups that are easily transported to picnics, the beach, and ball games. Or bring a summer-release natsuzake to your next BBQ—these are lower in ABV (13 to 15%), but because they are namas, they can still be bold and fruity. Some are even fizzy! We also love serving a genshu sake on the rocks.

Sake for Cold Weather

There's nothing like a steaming cup of sake on a dreadfully cold day, with everyone gathered around a pot roast or a *tsukune nabe* (meatball hot pot). We find that sakes that are full of umami or rice flavors, or have been aged, are great candidates for warming. Kimotos and yamahais have a tart acidity when warmed, and many junmais, especially ones that have been aged (including taruzake), have notes of spices and mushroom if served warm.

Debunking the Myth: Warm Sake Is Not Bad Sake

Nearly every day, we get asked, "Is warm sake bad?" Many people have clearly had bad experiences with sake served warm. It is such a shame, because the answer is NO!—one of the pleasures of sake is the way you can enjoy it with the changing of the seasons. It is really a unique beverage because of its ability to be enjoyed at temperatures ranging from ice-cold to warm and cozy.

How to Warm Sake

What actually happens when we warm sake? Its sweetness is enhanced because sugars are released. Heating a sake also smooths out any bitterness, which can make it taste mild and feel silky as it travels down your throat. And heating can open up different aromas that were less detectable when the sake was chilled. Warming can release savory or nutty fragrances—so let's go for it!

Step	Method
1	Transfer the sake to a *tokkuri* (sake flask) or glass beaker.
2	Fill a pot at least halfway with water and bring the water to a boil, then remove the pot from heat.
3	Place a thermometer (meat thermometers work well) in the sake and put the vessel in the pot of hot water. Wait for the thermometer to reach 105° to 120°F.
4	Remove the vessel from the water bath.
5	Pour the sake into ceramic cups.

PRO TIP: A word of caution—we don't recommend warming sake to temperatures over 120°F. Heating sake to just above this temperature can make it taste sharp and harsh. Warming it to 105° to 120°F is just enough to open up the savory flavors that are present in the sake, while ensuring that the sake cup will still feel comfortable in your hands (not scalding hot).

SERVEWARE

The world of sakeware is another aspect that is fun to explore. The material and shape of your sake cup can greatly affect your experience. Sake cups and carafes are mainly made of ceramic, glass, or wood. Different materials offer their own unique benefits and drawbacks—read on to learn about the various styles and specific purpose for each piece.

Ceramic

Ceramic is the original material for sake vessels, including cups and carafes. The reason why they still hold up as the ideal material for sake drinking is that they are practical (you can easily see the color of the sake and they are easy to wash) and aesthetically pleasing (thanks to Japan's long history of pottery making and its love affair with ceramics).

Ochoko is a traditional straight-sided sake cup that holds about two ounces. It is white on the outside and often has a blue bull's-eye pattern on the bottom of the cup (the illustration below shows a kikichoko, a type of ochoko with blue rings used for tasting). This blue pattern, contrasted against the white, allows you to observe the color and viscosity of the sake inside. You may encounter ochoko at sushi restaurants—it is one of the most common sake cups used in Japan. A ceramic sake cup can also feel much more pleasurable against the lips than a glass one. In addition to offering a softer, more natural feel while sipping, ceramic seems to take on the temperature of the sake itself more easily than glass.

Carafes made of ceramic are called *tokkuri.* These are ideal for serving warm and room temperature sakes. You can put a *tokkuri* directly into a hot water bath to warm your sakes!

PRO TIP! If you want to enjoy your sake warm, preheat ceramic vessels by filling them with hot water for a couple of minutes, then discard the hot water and fill your cups with warm sake.

Glass

With newer, more fragrant styles of sake like fruity ginjos and lively namas, the use of glass vessels has come to the forefront. When tasting, glass is as functional as ceramic cups, offering familiarity to a new sake drinker.

Like ceramic, glass is great for tasting. Clear glass allows you to observe the color and texture of the sake, especially if you look at the glass against a white surface. Glass carafes are ideal for cold sake service, like daiginjos and namas.

And for taking in aromatics that you might not have noticed in straight-sided vessels, a wine glass can't be beat. For effervescent sakes like namas and sparkling sakes, a flute glass is ideal, as otherwise the bubbles will dissipate quickly.

One of the main benefits of serving sake in glass is that almost everyone already owns wine glasses or glass tumblers. Enjoying sake doesn't mean you have to invest in a whole new set of serveware, which can be a hurdle for getting into sake.

Sake Flutes

We keep referring to sake flutes in this book—what exactly are they? Usually made of glass or ceramic, these vessels are thin and narrow and stand about 4 inches high. They have a solid base like a pint glass but are narrower and smaller in scale. They are ideal for cold sake. The often flared opening allows for better aeration, enhancing aromas more readily.

Wood

Small wooden cups and boxes are also traditional vessels for sake drinking. Although they are a bit unpractical, they still have their benefits and can be worth exploring if you'd care to do so. Although tasting in wood may not give you the true flavor of the sake, it can enhance the tasting experience in different ways, such as by adding an herbal aroma and seeing the liquid against a wooden surface. And, like ceramic, wood can deliver a pleasurable experience both aesthetically and in tactile ways.

Sake is sometimes served in a *masu* (cedar box). Masus were traditionally used to measure one serving of rice (180 ml) at the market. To prove to customers that they weren't being cheated, sake shop owners would measure sake into these boxes, and these then became serving vessels for sake. When you order a glass of sake at a bar or restaurant, you might get a tall glass inside the masu. In this case, the server will fill the glass and let the sake overflow into the masu (you should then pour the overflow back into the glass when it's empty). The overflow signifies plentifulness.

Because you can't identify the color and true aromas of a sake served in wood, it is not the ideal receptacle for serious note-taking. However, we've enjoyed the way in which stronger yamahai junmais and bodaimotos, especially when warmed, can play off the cedar smell of a masu. And if a sake that is tart or herbal is warmed, the aromatics of the wood can bring out those flavors. Wood is also great at keeping in the heat once a sake is warmed.

Recommendations for Vessels by Sake Style + Type

Sake	Vessel	Temperature	Why
Nama, ginjo, daiginjo, sparkling	Wine glass	Chilled	Can see color and clarity; stem keeps hands from warming up chilled sake; texture of sake is tight and crisp in glass
Junmai, honjozo	White ceramic ochoko	Room temperature or slightly chilled	Can see color and clarity; straight sides capture aromas of rice, custard, and yogurt; creamy, full-bodied texture feels good in the soft texture of ceramic
Kimoto, yamahai, koshu	White ceramic ochoko	Warmed to 110°F	Can see the color and clarity; warmed, the tart aromas are enhanced and the flavor is sweeter; ceramic stands up to the heat and feels good in the hand

STORING

One of the most frequently asked questions in our shop is, "How long will the sake keep after it's been opened?" As always, we are here to answer your burning questions.

Opened

If you open a bottle of pasteurized sake and don't finish it all in one sitting, simply recap it very tightly and put it back in the coolest part of your fridge. If you have a wine stopper with a vacuum pump, even better. At our bar, we replace the original lids with these stoppers after opening the bottle and then pump out the air between pours. The sake you put back in your fridge will keep for up to one week. After that, we love to use our old sakes for cooking.

For namas and nigoris, we recommend consuming the whole bottle in one sitting. Because the aromas in namas are quite unstable and can change very quickly (in just a few hours), it's best to commit to enjoying the whole bottle. Invite some friends over for a namafest and polish it off! We also recommend finishing a bottle of nigori in one sitting because over time, the rice particles can start to get a bit syrupy, and the sake will lose its original texture.

Sakes are much more forgiving than wine once opened. Once wines have been opened, they will start to turn into vinegar. And beers will fall flat in a matter of hours. Pasteurized sake, however, will retain its flavor and texture for one week after it's opened, as long as you cap it tightly and store it in the fridge. So the pressure is *not* on, and you can rest easy knowing you can enjoy your sake over the course of the week.

Sealed

Most sakes are pasteurized and will remain stable for up to two years after the bottling date as long as they are stored in a cool, dark place. And by *stable,* we mean that the flavors intended by the brewer are intact—the sake will not go bad and become hazardous for consumption. However, sakes stored for too long may end up tasting flat, express a less complex aroma, and/or look more golden in color. Since sake is brewed like beer and is intended to be enjoyed after bottling, we recommend that you buy sake with the mindset of buying beer. Think more along the lines of, "I'm getting this sake for a dinner party I'm going to next week," rather than, "I'm going to buy this sake and put it in my wine cellar for a few years."

Storage temperature and any exposure to light can speed up the deterioration of sake, which has no preservatives. So when in doubt (especially in the summer), we recommend storing it in the coolest corner of your refrigerator. If you want to drink the sake at room temperature or warm, remove it from the fridge one to two hours before serving.

Unpasteurized and nigori sakes are less stable and should be treated with more care. To determine if your sake is unpasteurized, look for the word *nama,* or unpasteurized, on the label. Many stores, including ours, keep their namas in the fridge and this can be a hint as to how you should store your sake once you get it home. Once you buy a nama, keep it in your fridge and try to enjoy it within a month or two—the sooner, the better.

Pasteurizing stops any potential fermentation and is typically administered before storage and then again before bottling. In namas and sakes that skip one or both of the pasteurizations, the flavors will be changing due to residual fermentation, which is why it is imperative to enjoy namas very soon after they are bottled. For nigoris, the rice particles, which are high in sugar, increase the rate of occurrence of bottle fermentation and therefore, like namas, should be enjoyed soon after purchase.

Spoilage

Sake can succumb to spoilage if it is too old or stored incorrectly. The main enemies of sake are light and heat. If the sake has been exposed to light or heat and you notice any of the following aromas or tastes, consider it spoiled!

- The sake smells like rotten eggs, compost, or burnt plastic or rubber.
- The sake tastes unusually bitter.
- The sake looks yellow and cloudy, but it's not a nigori or aged.

6

AFTERWORD

START YOUR EVERYDAY SAKE JOURNEY

Our sake journeys started two decades ago and continue to engage us in so many ways. What started out as, "This is delicious, what is it?" has led us to experiences from touching the soil of rice paddies in Shiga to calling up Harold McGee and learning about the components of umami. It is a fulfilling journey every day, and we are thrilled that you are now a part of it.

We hope that this book has given you the confidence to interact with sake in a new way. Pick up a sake on a shelf at your local bottle shop and read the bottle to recognize a few words on it. Compare a sake or two that are on a menu. Go to a local sake brewery in your own city or the next place you travel to and meet the brewer!

If you're feeling the sake spark, start a sake notebook and use the tips outlined in How to Taste Sake on page 100 to document your reactions. Note-taking is probably the most significant threshold you can cross to deepen your knowledge and clarify your preferences. When you take notes, you'll start to see patterns that help you home in on what you like. Whether it's in a little black notebook you designate for sake tasting or on your note-taking app on your phone, recording your impressions is the best thing you can do to start your sake journey. We have a staff member who started a spreadsheet with tasting notes and observations about the very first sake he tasted in 2019, and he still maintains it today at nearly 600 sakes!

Refer to chapter 2 for details on what to focus on when tasting sakes and how to taste for them. However, you may not always have the luxury to notate each one every time. In those instances, simply take note of the following:

Date of Tasting	
Sake Name	
Type/Style	
Brewery	
Region/Country	
Appearance	
Aroma	
Taste	
General Rating	

With lines for those items alone, you will document enough details to remember the sake should you wish to revisit it, and to give you a springboard for future tastings from that same brewery, region, or type.

If you do have time, print out and fill in the sake tasting template we have on our site at www.umamimart.com.

While it's ideal to take notes on what you're tasting, your sake journey starts and continues simply by enjoying sake and thinking about it. Off you go on your Everyday Sake journey!

FURTHER LEARNING AND READING

Classes

Sake School of America: Based in Los Angeles, this is the only program endorsed by the Sake Service Institute (SSI), the largest organization for sake sommelier (*kikizakeshi*) certification in Japan. They offer courses ranging from classes for the sake-curious (Sake Advisor) to those for advanced students (International Kikizakeshi). Classes are offered online and at the school in Los Angeles and New York.

Wine and Spirit Education Trust (WSET): Based in London, the Trust offers courses geared towards people in the beverage industry. Classes are available in cities around the world. Courses range from a few days to a few weeks long and include both a written and tasting exam.

The Sake Education Council: John Gauntner, who is based in Kamakura and is arguably the best-known sake educator teaching in English, teaches the certified Sake Professional Course all around the world. This is a great course for beginners and industry professionals alike.

The Sake Studies Center at Brooklyn Kura offers dynamic classes in person and online on the subject of sake. Additionally, they offer certification courses.

Reading

Exploring the World of Japanese Craft Saké (2022) by Nancy Matsumoto and Michael Tremblay

The Saké Handbook (2022) by John Gauntner

The Complete Guide to Japanese Drinks (2019) by Stephen Lyman and Chris Bunting

The Insider's Guide to Saké (1998) by Philip Harper

Visit umamimart.com for sake notes, brewery visit posts, and travels guides to Japan.

Join Our Club

Expand your horizons with Sake Gumi, Umami Mart's monthly sake club. Get curated bottles every month alongside tasting newsletters, food pairing suggestions, discounts, and invitations to member-only events. Join now at umamimart.com

GLOSSARY

Amazake (*ah-mah-zah-kay*): A nonalcoholic sake made with rice, water, and koji. It is sweet, high in umami (and probiotics), and enjoyed by children and adults alike.

Aruten (*ah-roo-ten*): Short for *arukoru tenka* (meaning "added alcohol"), the word *aruten* refers to the practice of adding distilled alcohol to sake. In large amounts, it is done to increase yield. In small amounts, it is done to add dimension, give the sake a silky texture, and draw out aromas.

Bodaimoto (*bo-die-moe-toe*): A highly acidic yeast starter that originated in the Shoryakuji Temple in Nara in the 1200s. It is made by combining *soyashi mizu* (water rich in lactic acid made by soaking uncooked rice in water at ambient temperatures), cooked rice, yeast, and koji. Versions using this method but not made at Shoryakuji Temple are referred to as *mizumoto*.

Daiginjo (*die-gin-joe*): A sake that is made using rice polished down to at least 50%.

Doburoku (*doe-boo-row-koo*): Considered the home brew of sake. It is made with a simpler style of fermentation where there is not the usual three-step addition of rice, koji, and water (*sandan jikomi*) to the starter. The result is a very thick brew—thicker than nigori—that's lower in alcohol than your typical sake.

Futsushu (*foot-sue-shoe*): Regular (table) sake that can be made with distilled alcohol, table rice, and additives.

Genshu (*ghen-shoe*): An undiluted or tank-strength sake. Sakes can naturally ferment to 18 to 20% ABV. To get down to 15%, brewers will add water to just-pressed sake.

Ginjo (*ghin-joe*): A sake that is made using rice polished down to at least 60%.

Honjozo (*hone-joe-zou*): A sake that has five ingredients: water, rice, yeast, koji, and distilled alcohol (up to 10% of the weight of the rice used to make the sake).

Ichi-go (*ee-chee-goe*): A single serving of sake, or 180 ml (6 fluid ounces).

Jukusei (joo-koo-say): A general term for maturation or aging; it can also refer to a sake that has aged for less than three years.

Junmai (*joon-ma-ee*): A sake that has just four ingredients: water, rice, yeast, and koji.

Kanpai (*kahn-pa-ee*): The Japanese phrase for "Cheers!" when toasting.

Karakuchi (*kah-rah-koo-chee*): A dry sake style.

Kijoshu (*kee-joe-shoe*): A sweet dessert sake that is made with a proportion of sake replacing brewing water.

Kimoto (*kee-moe-toe*): A yeast starter made by combining steamed rice, water, and koji into a mash by pounding them with poles. Lactic acid develops naturally, then yeast is added.

Koji (*koh-jee*): Rice inoculated with koji mold that is used in sake-making. Koji-inoculated rice looks like crumbly dried rice.

Koji mold spores: A fungal growth used in the production of various Japanese ferments, including those for sake, shochu, miso, and soy sauce. There are three main types: yellow (*Aspergillus oryzae*), which is commonly used for sake; white (*Aspergillus kawachii*); and black (*Aspergillus awamori*), which is used for shochu and awamori. To make sake, the spores, which resemble a fine greenish powder, are gently shaken onto steamed rice.

Koshu (*koh-shoe*): A sake that has been aged for at least three years.

Kurabito (*koo-rah-bee-toe*): Sake brewer.

Masu (*mah-sue*): Square cedar boxes that were traditionally used to measure one serving of rice (180 ml) at the market and are now used for drinking sake.

Maillard reaction: A chemical reaction between amino acids and reducing sugars that occurs at high temperatures; it's most typically associated with the browning of bread crusts and meats during baking or searing. This reaction occurs during the aging of sake at room temperature or higher, giving the sake a golden or amber color and caramel flavors.

Mizumoto (*mee-zoo-moe-toe*): See *Bodaimoto* (page 206).

Moromi (*moe-row-mee*): The main sake fermentation, where raw ingredients including rice, water, and koji are typically added in three stages with the moto.

Moto (*moe-toe*): The yeast starter used in sake-making; examples include bodaimoto, kimoto, and yamahai. It is also referred to as *shubo*.

Multiple parallel fermentation: A process that allows starch to convert to sugar and alcohol simultaneously by incorporating both yeast and koji.

Muroka (*moo-row-kah*): A sake that skips charcoal-filtering after pressing, sometimes resulting in a slightly yellow hue or heavier viscosity.

Nama (*nah-mah*), **Namazake** (*nah-mah-zah-kay*): Unpasteurized sake. Sake usually goes through two pasteurizations: one after pressing, and one after storage. Nama can refer to sakes that skip one or both pasteurizations.

Namachozo (*nah-mah-cho-zoh*): Sake that skips the first pasteurization (after pressing).

Namazume (*nah-mah-zoo-meh*): Sake that skips the second pasteurization (after storage).

Nigori (*nee-go-ree*): A sake that includes some sake lees, which can result in a cloudy appearance and sweeter flavor.

Nihonshu (*nee-hone-shoe*): The Japanese word for sake.

Ochoko (*oh-cho-koh*): Small ceramic cups used for drinking sake.

Sakamai (*sah-kah-ma-ee*): Rice used for sake-making.

Sake (*sah-kay*): A Japanese fermented beverage made from rice; the word *sake* is the generic term for alcohol in Japan, while *nihonshu* is the specific term for "Japanese sake." Outside of Japan, *sake* is used instead of *nihonshu*.

Sake kasu (*sah-kay-kah-sue*): Rice solids that are a by-product of sake-making. Also referred to as *lees.*

Sake Meter Value (SMV): Represented as a numerical value (typically ranging from –20 to +10), SMV refers to the amount of sugar present in a sake. Negative numbers denote more sugar, while positive numbers denote less.

Sandan jikomi (*sahn-dahn-jee-koh-mee*): Refers to the technique of adding rice, water, and koji in three stages during *moromi* (the main fermentation).

Seimaibuai (*say-ma-ee-boo-ah-ee*): The percentage of rice remaining after the grains are polished to make sake.

Shiboritate (*shee-boh-ree-tah-tay*): A sake that skips storage/maturation after pressing and is immediately bottled and released.

Shinpaku (*sheen-pah-koo*): The starchy core of a grain of rice.

Shochu (*show-choo*): A Japanese distilled alcohol typically distilled from rice, sweet potatoes, and barley. *Kasutori shochu* is a variety made with sake kasu.

Shubo (*shoo-bo*): Yeast starter, also referred to as *moto.*

Sokujo (*sow-koo-joe*): A yeast starter made by combining water, yeast, koji, lactic acid, and steamed rice. This is a modern method, and today 90% of all sake is made using this technique.

Souhaze (*sow-hah-zay*): A koji growth pattern that thoroughly covers the surface of the rice and goes inside with koji filaments, producing a richer, thicker style of sake.

Taruzake (*tah-roo-zah-kay*): Sake that is finished in cedar barrels for a few weeks, imparting a minty, herbal flavor.

Tokkuri (*toe-koo-ri*): A sake flask, typically ceramic.

Tokubetsu (*toe-koo-bet-sue*): Meaning "special" in Japanese, this type of sake is made with either rice that's been polished down to 60% or a special brewing method that the maker wants to highlight.

Tokuteimeishoushu (*toe-koo-tay-mayshow-shoe*): Premium sakes that are subject to requirements about ingredients and rice polishing. Koji rice must make up 15% of the total rice used to make the sake.

Tsukihaze (*tsue-key-hah-zay*): A koji growth pattern that results in sparse coverage on the surface of the rice grains but full growth inside for a lighter, elegant style of sake.

Umami (*oo-mah-mee*): The "fifth taste," after sweet, salty, bitter, and sour. The term refers to savory, nutty, meaty flavors detected in foods and drinks that are high in glutamates and nucleotides.

Usunigori (*oo-sue-nee-go-ree*): A light nigori.

Yamahai (*yah-mah-ha-ee*): A yeast starter that combines steamed rice, water, and koji—it's similar to kimoto, but made without pounding the mash with poles. Lactic acid develops naturally, then yeast is added.

Yeast: In sake-making, yeast converts the glucose into alcohol and produces carbon dioxide, and esters. Brewers choose different strains of yeast depending on their stamina, ability to work at different temperatures, and aroma. Most brewers use strains managed by the Nihon Jozo Kyoukai (Brewing Society of Japan), while a minority uses proprietary, flower-derived, or ambient strains.

ACKNOWLEDGMENTS

We would have never imagined the amount of support and expertise needed to put this book together. The knowledge and enthusiasm of our worldwide sake community gave us the confidence to complete this book. We would like to thank all of our sake colleagues and teachers who have patiently answered our questions and partook in hours of musings, including Yoshihiro Sako of Den Sake Brewery, Shuso Imada of the Sake and Shochu Association in Tokyo, Tamiko Ishidate, Izumi Motai of Takara Sake, Timothy Sullivan of the Sake Studies Center, Jesse Pugach of Fifth Taste, John Gauntner, Mayuko Kita of Kita Shuzo, Keizo Ishida of Matsuse Shuzo, Miho Imada of Imada Shuzo, and Shinichi Washino. Shout-out to Ian Rittmaster for all the fun acronyms you came up with and to Jenny Eagleton who may or may not have come up with the brilliant "Ginjo as Goldilocks" reference after a few glasses of sake at our bar. And a very special thank-you to Kerry Jo Rizzo, who imparted her razor-sharp edits at the last hour.

We would like to thank Chris Brockway and Bridget Leary of Broc Cellars, who are always so generous and willing to share their expertise on wine and its current landscape. And when we felt misguided on how to describe everything we were tasting, we were honored to speak to Harold McGee, who is effortlessly engaging and clear in his explanation about food and science.

This book was a mirage, at best, since we started Umami Mart as a blog back in 2007, and our book agent, Jonah Straus, made it into a dream. From there, Jennifer Sit, our editor, made it into a reality. Thank you for pushing us to dig deep and unearth some uncharted discussion. We are a fly-by-the-seat-of-our-pants kind of duo, and we are so grateful that Ian Dingman, our designer who has the patience of a saint, made this book into something that someone can actually understand. And, yes, we knew, oh, we knew, that Anders Arhoj, our illustrator and so much more, had to be involved. He has never steered us off course, no matter how difficult the terrain. We always make it, somehow . . . our vision and friendship in one piece.

Back on the store front, we would like to thank De'Andre Crenshaw and all of our staff, past and present, who kept the shop open and running while we were meeting deadlines and taking Zoom calls in the back room. While we hope the adventure will continue beyond our doors, our shop remains our clubhouse; and our staff, family.

Thank you to our mentor, Dick Schliesmann, who helped us secure a small loan to load up on Christmas inventory back in 2013—and who still comes by on random Tuesdays to remind us that a "penny saved is a penny earned." We hope we've made him proud and that "the horse has NOT left the barn" for this book.

And finally, thank you to our community, in Oakland and beyond, for sticking by us since day one and supporting our little Japanese drink shop. You make our business possible.

Yoko

Wow, we wrote a book! I am so grateful to have Kayoko as my partner in crime for this challenging project. Thank you for being practical and honest every step of the way. I am always in awe of your ability to be objective and decisive. I cannot imagine doing this with anyone else. And whatever's next, I'll see you there.

Anders, thank you for your incredible talent, generosity, and laser focus. But most of all, thank you for your friendship.

John, thank you for being my bumble bee watch partner for life. My favorite part of every day is coming home to you.

And finally, thank you to my mom, Cindy, Maria, and Mei.

Kayoko

I'm not sure which one of us thought writing this book would be a good idea, but Yoko and I can tackle anything together so I knew it would turn out just fine. Did it??? Thank you, Yoko, for being the best work wife, friend, and companion. You inspire me every day!

Thank you to the Lopes family, Christi, and Erin for your encouragement of me and this book. Anders, meet ya at our pied-à-terre in Kanazawa!

Growing up in a restaurant, I learned all about hard work and community from my parents at Sushi Kuni. Thank you to Baba, Jiji (the original Junmai Guy), and Kei for the lifetime of culinary inspiration and small business spirit.

To Mion and Johnny, thank you for making each day brighter. You are my everything.

INDEX

K

L

M

N

O

P

R

S

T

Clarkson Potter/Publishers
An imprint of the Crown Publishing Group
A division of Penguin Random House LLC
1745 Broadway
New York, NY 10019
clarksonpotter.com
penguinrandomhouse.com

Library of Congress Cataloging-in-Publication Data
Names: Kumano, Yoko author | Akabori, Kayoko author | Arhøj, Anders illustrator
Title: Everyday sake : the go-to guide to choosing + pairing / Yoko Kumano and Kayoko Akabori; illustrations by Anders Arhoj.
Description: New York : Clarkson Potter/Publishers, [2026] | Includes index. |
Identifiers: LCCN 2025025068 | ISBN 9780593799734 hardcover | ISBN 9780593799741 ebook
Subjects: LCSH: Rice wines—Handbooks, manuals, etc. | Food and wine pairing—Handbooks, manuals, etc. | LCGFT: Handbooks and manuals
Classification: LCC TP579 .K86 2026 | DDC 641.2/2—dc23/eng/20251118
LC record available at https://lccn.loc.gov/2025025068

ISBN 978-0-593-79973-4
Ebook ISBN 978-0-593-79974-1

Editor: Jennifer Sit
Editorial assistant: Elaine Hennig
Designer: Ian Dingman
Production designer: Christina Self
Production editor: Terry Deal
Production: Philip Leung
Compositors: Hannah Hunt, Zoe Tokushige
Copy editor: Judith Sutton
Proofreaders: Nicole Ramirez, Clare Ling
Indexer: Eldes Tran
Publicist: David Hawk
Marketer: Chloe Aryeh

Manufactured in China

10 9 8 7 6 5 4 3 2 1

First Edition

The authorized representative in the EU for product safety and compliance is Penguin Random House Ireland, Morrison Chambers, 32 Nassau Street, Dublin D02 YH68, Ireland, https://eu-contact.penguin.ie.

YOKO KUMANO and **KAYOKO AKABORI** are the founders of Umami Mart, a Japanese drinks store in Oakland, California. Childhood friends from Cupertino, they started a food blog called *Umami Mart* in 2007 as a way to stay in touch (and deflect boredom) from their cubicle jobs in Tokyo and New York. After moving back to the Bay Area, they opened their shop in downtown Oakland in 2012. Umami Mart started as a barware and kitchen tools store before expanding to sake and spirits, and it now focuses on sake education through classes and a monthly club. The shop has been featured in *The New York Times*, *Wirecutter*, and *New York* magazine.